The Eighteen Holes of Success

Wall Street Edition

Schenk Enterprises
116 Kings Creek Circle
Rehoboth Beach, Delaware 19971

ISBN: 0-9704811-0-1

Library of Congress Catalog Card Number: 00-192125

Printed in the United States of America

ABOUT THIS BOOK

If we are lucky, we get to try our hand at a wide variety of challenging occupations as we go through life. When work and fun become one. During the three year journey of this book I became an author, a publisher, a graphic designer, a photographer, and a student of the game I love. It only occasionally felt like work. But I had help.

After a year and a half, eighteen friends reviewed my first draft on their time and their dime. These generous minds took me through their thoughts on what to do with this book. I absorbed their ideas and went back to work. Those people opened my mind and I cannot thank them enough. They are: Chase Brockstedt, Jim Platner, Sam Ibrahim, David Barrios, Joe Dunn, Blase Cooke, Paul Saiz, Junius Tillery, Charles Call, Paul McDonough, Jeff Bradley, Gary Schenk, Jeff Schenk, Kevin Smith, Dave and Sandy Schenk, Betsi Fakler, Brian Dawson, and Ron Collins. Other friends and acquaintances sprinkled in a little brain candy here and there. Thank you all.

After another year or so, I met Brian McAndrew, an editor for *The Toronto Star* who had written a few books and offered his talent as an editor. He cleaned it up beautifully and asked for nothing in return. The awesome graphical artwork is the work of Darin Wardwell. He is the genius who brought the book to life. He's doing things on the web that can melt your mind. Thank you, gentlemen.

My wife, Bethany, simply inspired, supported, and believed. Thank you Mrs. Schenk.

CONTENTS

The spectacular putting green at the Robert Trent Jones Golf Club is a great place to start your round. Manassas, Virginia.

THE PRACTICE TEE – WARMING UP

I looked straight up at the gray, 25-story, stone building in downtown Baltimore. It looked more like a church than an office building. The revolving brass and glass door was still in motion and gently swept me inside. The lobby was huge with brass everywhere and worn marble floors. Old-school everything. The two-story atrium was filled with elaborately painted ceilings and golden fixtures suspended in air. It even smelled like church. The building was warm, hot actually. I could hear the steam hissing out of the antiquated heating system. If church is where we learn our most valuable lessons, this was church.

Majestic steps dominated the lobby. The thick metal handrails were polished smooth over the years by the sweaty palms of people like me. It made you want to do business the old fashioned way.

I pretended to know where I was going and avoided eye contact with the security guard. My destination was the 16th floor. Today, I was selling my business. A business founded seven years earlier that withstood the devastating droughts, predators, fears, and injuries encountered by all of the survivors. The rules of nature also apply to business. Only the strong survive.

Selling a business is an education within itself. I always envisioned a mega-corporation showing up with a check and escorting me to the door with a "you have built a nice business, we'll take it from here. Good luck to you." Nothing could be further from the truth. The formal process of selling a business is an emotional, excruciatingly detailed and complicated process.

Deep in my heart I was burned-out. I had lost my desire to drive the business forward but I had to keep that secret hidden in the bus locker of my soul. If the buyer knew how badly I was ready to punt they would have cut their offer in half and hoped I never returned their call. The business was thriving, but it had worn my corners round. The time had come for someone else to pull the wagon. Even if they pulled it five feet and struck oil I would have been happy for them. Genuinely.

The final details of the sale were documented in a binder that required two hands and a grunt to lift and included language that I henceforth, whereby, barely understood-eth. What I did know was that somewhere in this building, five or ten people were milling around a conference table collating and binding for the kickoff of signatures scheduled to begin this morning. The last time I was this excited I still believed in Santa Claus.

I learned in those seven years that deals could crash a thousand different ways. Today's deal still had a long way to go. Until the money was wired, I still had a company to run. On the elevator ride up, the emotion from the realization that I had accomplished something very special came over me. The business was the classic story of "let's start a business out of the apartment." When we started, I did not own a kitchen table. Our third client wanted to meet at our office, so I invited him over to sit at a table I didn't have. Somehow, we figured something out. We always did. We had no choice. Building the business was the tuition we paid to learn some of life's greatest lessons.

The lights illuminated the elevator's brass panel, **9**...**10**...*and just before the 16th floor light signaled the end of my journey, my last thought was that I could not wait to tee it up. The doors opened, and I stepped into my retirement.*

I love golf and business with the same passion. Business and golf are connected at the soul.

We entertain clients on the golf course, and we conduct business with selected golf partners. At work, our mind drifts to the shot that felt perfect. Walking up the fairway, proudly preparing for your tap-in birdie putt, the win-win solution for the deal becomes clear. As the perfectly stroked putt gently melts into the hole, everything seems to come together. Golf exposes our business character, and we learn some of life's greatest lessons on the golf course.

We take risks at work, and we gamble on the course. If you make unwise decisions or fail to execute, you lose money. Plain and simple. Golf and business are inseparable.

Business is part sport, part war, and part chess. No matter what you do for a living, you know you can improve your performance. When the check clears or the contract gets signed, you think: "How can I do that again?"

Golf is part sport, part war, and part chess. It can amplify your success with one swing and destroy you with the next. Golf can be as fragile as a Christmas ornament. No matter how long you have been playing, you know you can play better. After playing a great round, every golfer asks: "How can I do that again?"

What are the *18 Holes of Success*? I have designed a unique 18-hole golf course. Each hole offers techniques that will help you attain your definition of success. Golf teaches us that personal improvement can span a lifetime. After you play my course and embrace the lessons, you will begin to enjoy your round of golf more and, most importantly, experience success sooner at work and in your personal life. And because the beauty of nature is a requirement for every round of golf, I have included a few personal photographs from some of the world's most spectacular golf courses.

Why should you listen to me? While you have been at work, I have been researching your success. If I'm awake, I'm smiling. The first thing I do every morning (or afternoon) when I wake up is laugh out loud. I am not the wealthiest, the best looking, or most athletic person, but I just may be the happiest. I spent two and a half years answering the question "How and why did all of this happiness fall into my lap?" The answers are *The 18 Holes of Success*.

I am **sure** this book can help you. The more I studied, the more I saw the game of golf teaching the same secrets. It was then that I decided "golf course architecture" would be for me. I would design a golf course that would teach people life's secrets to success.

The 18 Holes of Success are your blue prints for the following:

Fulfilling relationships. Happiness cannot be celebrated on an island. This book will make you more attractive to the opposite sex and a welcome addition to any group or business venture. Until you understand that relationships begin with your ability to draw people to you, love and support will have to be coerced. Fulfilling relationships will find **you** if you live by these *18 Holes of Success*.

Freedom. A stress-free world is utopia. Follow the lessons on the following pages, and you can take control of your destiny. Fate is a myth. Control of your environment, emotions, and schedule are keys to happiness. Finding freedom in your daily grind is possible if you are willing to make the investment.

Passion. Living with a passion will introduce so much excitement into your world that you will not have time for the normal distractions of boredom, complacency or self-doubt.

Challenge. Because the destination is the journey, challenging yourself throughout your life is a way to guarantee success. Challenging your fears and weaknesses is a part of success.

Achievement of Goals. Testing yourself against your desires tests your will. You add confidence as you believe that no goal is unattainable. Attainment of goals maximizes your abilities.

Faith and a spiritual connection. We experience miracles every day. The spirit of humanity lies in this magical connection. *The 18 Holes of Success* will help you believe in the faith of a greater purpose.

Satisfaction. Winning is a form of satisfaction. Personal achievements in athletics, competition and business help us live with a smile. So does satisfaction from helping others and living out your dreams.

Contentment. Relaxation that accompanies success is sweet. You never have trouble sleeping, and your life feels fulfilled on every level.

Money. The best thing about money is that it can buy you time. More money lets you have the time to do the things that make you happy. Nice things are nice to have, however, material items are only a small piece of your worth. This book will show you how to make more money so you can share your success with others.

Now that you know the pin placements, here's what the yardage book offers to help you play your best.

The Course Layout. The course opens with mental preparation and planning holes. The first three holes are critical to your preparation for success. Holes four through nine discuss the tools and techniques that you will need to use on your journey. You will then have the opportunity to reflect in the grillroom before heading out for the back nine. Holes ten through sixteen present strategies for achieving success sooner and avoiding the inevitable hazards on your way. Holes seventeen and eighteen are this course's signature holes and are the two most important characteristics of every successful person.

Because you are here on the practice tee, I know you are serious about your success. You may not yet have all of the answers, but with the help of others, the answers are easier to find. You are willing to make changes in your life that will speed your success. Those two qualities tell me you already have a low handicap in the game of success.

Course Tips. After you finish your bucket of balls and stroke a few putts, walk to the first tee with the thought, "I will learn something on every hole I play." Challenge yourself to play these holes in all of your life's dealings. You will never be rained out or have to wait for a tee time. Let these *18 Holes of Success* become a part of your life.

You're next on the tee and I hope you enjoy my course.

"If just some of the sensible principles that keep businessmen out of trouble in their day to day affairs were applied to their golf game, their handicaps would drop drastically."
- Greg Norman, PGA Golfer and British Open Champion

1st Tee ➡

Confidence is required for your approach to the second green of Big Horn's Canyon Course. Palm Springs, California.

NUMBER 1 - POSITIVE MIND

I would rather be a poor man who thinks he's rich than a rich man who thinks he's poor. I would rather laugh all day and shoot a 98 than be miserable shooting 78. What matters is not where you are, but where you *think* you are.

Like most rounds of golf, the first hole can set the tone for the rest of your round. For that reason, I have chosen *Positive Mind* as my first hole. A positive mind is essential on your journey through the uncharted terrain, blind shots, difficult lies, and other hazards that you encounter along your life's *18 Holes of Success*.

On this hole you will see the immediate benefits of a positive mental state. It is a short hole that plays slightly downhill, has a wide fairway with no traps or hazards, and a large green. It's an easy opening hole to get your round started. Walking off this green you will see yourself as one of the lucky people on this earth. I'll drop the positive energy magnet in your pocket so people will gravitate to you instead of away from you. You will learn the immediate benefits of a positive mind and you can have it all by the time you get to the second tee.

So what exactly are the benefits of a positive mind? The list is long, but here's a start.

Happiness. How happy you are is a direct reflection of how you view yourself, the world around you and how you fit into that world. Only you can limit your happiness. Take off the governor, there's no speed limit on happiness.

Confidence. A positive mind forces you to believe in yourself. You cannot influence the world until you believe you have a significant contribution to make to yourself, your family, your career and, most importantly, your success. A positive mind is your internal strength to believe in yourself.

The ability to produce. A positive mental state is the most productive emotional environment. Internal positive energy will produce more, push you to work harder, summon greatness from yourself and everyone around you and open your mind to learn from everyone and everything. You will increase the enjoyment of what you are doing and work will seem less like work. This, combined with your sweat, makes you unstoppable.

A consistent, pleasant view of the world. A positive mind reminds you that you cannot control the world but you can control how the world views you and how you view the world. Pleasant is attractive.

A positive mind is a powerful force. It can overcome any obstacle and solve any problem. Do not underestimate the influence a positive mind can have. It's quite contagious and, unlike Visa and American Express, it is accepted everywhere. A positive mind overshadows every other first impression.

Now that you see the importance of a positive mind, how can you train your mind to think and stay positive?

Wear rose-colored glasses. Recognize that what you have is enough, and what you are striving for is gravy. Your worst day is a thousand people's best day. There will always be someone blessed with more money, charisma, intelligence or physical gifts than you have been given. However, **significantly** more people have less than you. A lot less. The fact that you can read is a gift that 25 percent of the world has not been given. Reminding yourself of all the gifts you have is the foundation for a positive mind. Be thankful for the opportunity to chase your dream and wear your gratitude on the surface of your personality.

The most important lesson that my parents taught me while growing up in South Georgia was how much we had to be thankful for. My brothers and sister and I were never allowed to be victims. We were taught at a very young age that where we found ourselves at any point in life is largely a result of our own decisions. We, after all, had the best of everything. A family that loved us, a roof over our head, and plenty of food. What else do you need to be happy?

I recently had the opportunity to holiday in South Africa, and I survived an emotional head-on collision with the strength of a positive mind. The drive across the African bush from Johannesburg to Sun City is a two-hour journey that exposed a level of poverty I never knew existed. The beautiful countryside is dotted with tin homes that are constructed with scrap corrugated tin sheets held together with all the complexity of a child's temporary backyard fort. Dirt floors and no running water. Entire families were sitting in the small rectangle of shade created by the tin house, the only relief from the baking African sun. We rode in silence as we tried to comprehend what life must be like in these living conditions.

*Once in Sun City, my wife and I settled into a restaurant and had an incredible experience with our waiter, William. He lived in one of these homes, but his enthusiasm for life was truly inspirational. In seven years, he had been promoted from dishwasher, to cook, to waiter, and he was enthusiastic about his inevitable advancement in the restaurant chain of command. The pride he displayed in his job, his friendly disposition, his professional attitude, his respect for his co-workers and managers and his sense of humor in light of the living conditions and general poverty of the region was an unforgettable personification of the positive mental spirit. I had never experienced anything like that, until the next day, when I met my assigned caddie, Floyd. He rode a bus 45 minutes, each way, to **possibly** have the opportunity to caddie for the equivalent of 10 American dollars. In the 100-degree heat he displayed the same pride, enthusiasm and happiness with his career and lot in life that I had seen the night before in William. How could these people with so little be so rich in spirit? My wife and I now have a family term that we keep close. During our mirages of stress or frustration, the simple term "Tin House" commands immediate silence out of respect for the people who have so little but simply choose not to complain.*

A positive mind is a noble choice.

"You can complain because roses have thorns or you can rejoice because thorns have roses."
-English proverb

Remove all jealousy from your life. Jealousy is self-destructive and impossible to hide. Not being able to be genuinely happy for the success of others is an indication of something missing from your life. Jealousy is the defeated soul admitting it has lost. The success of others should motivate you to believe that your success is inevitable.

Laugh hard every chance you can. Laughter is the best technique for retaining your spirit of youth. Even if you aren't the one telling the jokes or can't seem to fire off witty one-liners, you can still be the first to laugh at those who are being funny. Nothing will draw people to you more than genuine laughter. Laughter is contagious.

Avoid the "grass is greener" mentality. It is a sign of discontent, and it is not true anyway. Positive people are content with themselves and believe that tomorrow will bring new opportunities, challenges and rewards. They see laying blame as a waste of time and accept failure as part of the territory when conquering results and progress.

Use "No" like a four-letter word. You will be avoided if you are always the first one to say "no" or consistently have reasons why things should not be done. Difficult decisions are part of the leadership landscape. Do not let them deplete your positive energy. Practice saying "yes"; and when saying "no", explain why you did to maintain an environment of creativity. How you say "no" is a dead giveaway to your state of mind.

Be able to follow. Listening and taking direction from others is a way to learn and removes know-it-all habits that can easily accumulate. Team-oriented people are positive thinkers. It is easier to get help when you need it if you support the ideas of others and maintain a constructive attitude. If you manage others, work *with* people as opposed to replacing people. Positive thinkers are in the minority, so put yourself in the expensive seats just by changing your attitude.

Recognize that your mental state is completely up to you. Optimism is an aura that people feel, and you can have it if you want it. The main barrier to a positive mind is not accepting that you have 100 percent control over the state of your attitude. You do. Is your glass half empty or half full? I can't decide which full glass I'm going to drink from next.

Get out of the ivory tower. Return all phone calls and be accessible to everyone. Do not hide from anyone or anything and never point out a problem that you are not willing to solve.

"When choosing a partner, always choose the optimist"
- Tony Lema, professional golfer

A positive mind will help you conquer the difficult 8th hole of the Gary Player Country Club and Spa. Sun City, South Africa.

Use positive words and phrases. Be the first person to say something positive about every situation. A sense of humor is always a welcome guest. The world can certainly use more "Please," "Thank You," and "How can I help?" Negative energy encourages additional negative energy.

Q) If you come out of the movies and you notice that one of your tires is flat, you:

    a) Complain about your terrible luck

    b) Rejoice because you have 3 good tires left

    c) Rejoice because your car wasn't stolen

    d) Rejoice because you actually have a car

    e) Rejoice because you are not blind and could actually see the movie

A) B through E

Recognize **all** of your good fortune and struggles become a thing of the past.

"Keep your face to the sunshine and you cannot see the shadow."
- Helen Keller, deaf and blind author and public speaker

It is impossible to play golf well without a positive frame of mind.

Golf can make you want to hit yourself. Hard. A positive mind will remove the frustration. One way to do this is to remember your good shots, not your bad shots. Frustration is a significant barrier to your success on the golf course.

Slow down. Sometimes we get so caught up in playing golf in three and a half hours that we rush what is supposed to be relaxing. Don't play like you've got a cab waiting. Try to enjoy the day, the companionship, and the pure beauty and peace of the golf course.

Your best rounds are played when you are in a positive state of mind. When you find your zone and the hole looks like a bathtub and the fairway looks as wide as a parking lot, it **always** coincides with a positive mind and the belief that you can do no wrong. Are you playing well because of your positive mind or is your positive mind a result of you playing well? In this case, the chicken came before the egg. Bring your positive mind to every round you play.

Your frame of mind is completely and entirely in your control. Your attitude is up to you. Life is a series of choices and this is one of them. Golf is a game. Play it that way. Let it be fun and you will play better.

The ultimate goal is for the people you are playing with to want to play with you again. My goal for the people in my group is for them to shoot their career round, have the most fun, and somehow associate that with me.

"I shrug my shoulders to relax them. Then I try to remember the best shot I ever hit with whatever club I have in my hand."
- Fred Couples, Professional Golfer and
Masters Champion

The fall colors surround your destination. Congressional Country Club's welcoming 5th green. Washington, DC.

NUMBER 2 - WHAT'S YOUR TARGET?

Without a target, you will miss every time. The biggest mistake that you can make is taking action without a clear, well-defined target. Most of us have only a fuzzy definition of what we want out of life. Setting goals and realistic activities to achieve those goals clarifies your personal vision and guarantees that you will not waste time.

"This year we plan to run and shoot. Next season we hope to run and score."
-Billy Tubbs, NCAA basketball coach

The single purpose of this hole is to convince you of the absolute necessity of written goals. Before you select your club on this tee, take a look at the layout of the hole and decide exactly where you want to be for your next shot.

Here, you will learn why the most talented business minds motivate themselves (and their careers) along an action plan of how and when they will realize their desires. We will study the pin placement sheet, and you will see that without a clear definition of destinations, progress is haphazard, and your activities support your latest whim. After you toss a little grass in the air to check the wind, you will see that defining your personal goals will reduce your fear of failure and give you an immediate sense of self-worth. You will then see yourself as a work in process at a specific point on your blueprint to success. In life and golf, you must not take a swing until you know exactly where your shot must land.

Written goals work magic. Your dreams become goals when you write them down. A goal is a wish on paper. Documenting where you want to go is the first step toward making any serious commitment to an accomplishment. Deciding you want to paint murals from the porch of your million-dollar beach home will not make it happen overnight. However, it can happen as a part of your predetermined, long-term strategy. Every business, project, family, and individual that is impassioned about success must have a documented goal strategy that is easily accessible for review at a moment's notice. How many sets of written goals do you have for those areas of your life? The popular answer seems to be none. I resigned from a board of directors because, not only did they not have a written plan or mission statement, they refused to develop one. Check please.

Why is goal-planning missing in most of our lives? Goal-setting gets treated like your least favorite chore because of the fear of accountability, commitment, or failure. Goals are the cornerstone of accountability and commitment, and five seconds after you identify your personal targets, you will wonder how you ever got out of bed without them.

Goal-setting is not a natural act. Identifying goals always seems to be someone else's job. Setting goals is something we are never taught. In 16 years of formal education, goal-setting was, unfortunately, never mentioned. By documenting your goals you will instantly feel smarter, make better decisions, and be more attractive to the opposite sex because you now have something of value to share. Goal-setting will have that strong of an effect on you.

Your goals become your personal report card. Think of the impact your school report cards had when you were growing up. A few traumatic experiences come to mind very quickly. School report cards are everyone's first goal document. The goal was to exceed each area of study; and the report card measured your success toward achieving that goal. It also came with the additional stress of publicly sharing your success (or failure) with parents, siblings, and friends. School without a report card is nothing more than recess.

This chapter is about putting a personal report card back in your life. You get to pick the classes, and no one is going to mail your parents a copy. In fact, keeping your goals from the general public is one way to eliminate the negative feedback from others. However, once you define them and start achieving them, you most likely will want to share them with your close friends and family. Add a yearly or quarterly report card to your life and I guarantee you will accomplish more than you ever have before. The bell has rung and recess is over.

"You must have long-range goals to keep you from being frustrated by short-range failures."
-Thomas A. Edison, inventor of the light bulb and phonograph

Now that we agree that determining a target is step number one, how do we go about doing it? You can do this any way you want, but here is a suggestion. Get some paper and a pen. Right now, really. Set 8 to 12 goals every year. (Last year I accomplished 5 of my 10 goals.) Identify 2 long-term goals that you want to achieve in the next 5 years. Specify 2 business goals, 2 financial goals, 2 self-improvement goals, 2 family goals, and 2 goals that are personal to you. Painfully easy, but awkward getting started.

Develop your goals based on your <u>desired</u> lifestyle. Do not let your job dictate your lifestyle. Define your targets the other way around. Determine your lifestyle goals first, and then wrap your business goals around them. What are your life's goals? To have a flexible schedule? To spend more time with your family? To travel? To retire early?

The power is in the details. Write your goals in as much detail as possible and visualize yourself actually accomplishing them. The next, and most important, step is to put them where you have to look at them every day. Try to read them every day and not less than once a week. To guide you, they must be fresh in your mind. How often you read them is also a direct measure of your desire. Your plan then becomes the basis for all of your decisions. Your actions will support only the attainment of your goals. The plan is now written down and fresh in your mind, so attack it with a passion and a positive mind.

You **do** know what you want, so this is the easy part. When you get started, look at the clock and I will bet that in less than 30 minutes you will have a set of goals that will motivate you and give you an instant feeling of satisfaction. You have defined your life's purpose in less time than it takes to get a pizza.

"Be decisive. A wrong decision is generally
less disastrous than indecision."
- Bernhard Langer, Professional Golfer and Masters Champion

Complete the following for each one of your goals (and feel free to write in this book, it is yours):

I would like to:

_____

Before I can get this done I have to:

_____

I will achieve this by doing the following:

_____

I will get this done by the following date:

_____

"If you only had six months to live, what would you do, and if you're not doing that now, why not?"

- Anonymous

After you determine your targets, redefine them at least once a year. Use your birthday to make a list of things that you want to do before your next birthday. Use the New Year's resolution tradition to review last year's goals and set this year's. Be accountable to yourself. Review your success and failure and ask the question, "Why?" The answers are usually easy.

Finally, set realistic goals that are attainable with hard work and creativity. Create a sense of urgency and motivation. Your goals are your transition plan to your success.

A specific list of goals surrounding your career is necessary if you are serious about improving. At work, know what the goals are for the entire organization. Communicate with your boss and your boss's boss. Incorporate their goals into your goals. Make sure your activities support the company's mission, not just yours. There is nothing worse than doing a great job at something nobody cares about.

If you have employees, make sure that they have a **written** measure of success or specific goals that they must achieve. Manufacturing facilities and sales people typically have quotas, but all employees need to have quantifiable, measurable goals to maximize their talent. These goals need to be monitored on a regular basis to chart success but more importantly to teach employees to be accountable for their written goals.

Failure. After your goals are defined, what do you do when you fail to reach them? First, expect to miss a few of your goals. If you accomplish all of your goals, you set them too low. How you deal with missing a target is up to you, but I choose not to beat myself up as long as I have exerted every effort. Recommit yourself, change your preparation activities, or give yourself more time. Do not view this as failure but a slight change of plans. Then, change your plans.

Sometimes you realize that a goal is unattainable and, therefore, has no business on your list. For instance, one goal I set for myself 6 years ago was to dunk a basketball. Silly to you, but tomahawking one in traffic is every round baller's dream. Mine included. I am 6' 1" and a lot of people shorter than that can slam. I lost some weight and began practicing with a volleyball. I lifted weights and put up posters of a few of the NBA's most ferocious dunks in my exercise room. My imaginary poster was me coming out of nowhere to dunk on 3 or 4 of my Monday night boys and actually having them stop the

CONDITION

game and look at each other as I trot down court pretending not to notice. Early in the process, the boys howled as I pinned the volleyball on the underside of the rim during my wait for the next game. They stopped laughing when the volleyball started bouncing to halfcourt off the back of the rim and didn't say a thing when I started dunking it with authority. When I switched to working with a basketball, I just could not hold it firmly enough during my approach to the rim. Knowing I could not jump high enough to dunk with two hands and realizing that my hands were done growing, I adjusted my goal to: dunk a volleyball. I checked it off the list and never thought about it again. In some cases, your limitations win. Change your goals after you have done your best.

A spectator said, "I don't think you understand. You have to hit the hole, not the car!"
- Mary Dwyer, LPGA golfer, after hitting the car that would be awarded for a hole in one.

On the golf course the hole is the obvious target, but not the only target. Do not forget friendship, improvement, challenge, and relaxation.

Golf is a series of little tournaments made up of shots. Before you can win each of those tournaments, you've got to ask yourself, "What is the target?" Define a specific goal: "I'm aiming on the tree line, on the left side, 40 yards to the right of that sand trap."

Commit to the specific target in mind before you begin your backswing. Recognize that this is an additional focus task and does take an extra mental exercise. Once you have done your best to find your target, trust the swing. Having a specific target makes it easier to believe in the swing or putt.

A bullseye is required for your approach into the 14th green on Blackwolf Run's Meadow Valleys Course. Kohler, Wisconsin.

Finding your target in golf is unnatural. In basketball you look at the rim before you shoot your shot. In football and baseball you watch the ball as you catch it. Golf is the only sport where you aim for a target that you do not see as you hit the ball. You are looking down at the ball and aiming to a blind target ninety degrees directly to your left (or right for left handers). You cannot see the target, you have to "feel" where it is. A good last swing thought is to pretend that you are **playing in the dark**, and forget about looking for the ball as it leaves the swing. The darkness image is a mental exercise to help you stay with your shot and keep your head down.

To define your line stand behind the ball, pick your line of flight, and find a target a foot or two in front of the ball. A blade of grass or a leaf. Now fire the ball over the new target. Your mind has to have an imaginary target that you can visualize and "feel" although you are not looking at it. When you are putting, always putt toward a break and not toward the hole. We all have a tendency during our stroke to second guess our confidence and think: "Wait a minute! I can't putt it there... The hole's over there!" Putt to your target line. Every putt is a straight putt as it leaves your putter.

Golf is a delicate balance between offense and defense. You play both on each swing. Factoring in where you do not want to hit it is just as much a part of your target as where you do want to hit it.

I hit better shots when I call my shots. With good friends, I'll say, "I'm going to hit this 3 iron just in front of the green and let it bounce up. Check it out." I have hit more shots that I have called because I now have something specific in mind. Its obnoxious to call all your shots out loud, but call them to yourself and I bet you will hit more than your share.

"Art said he wanted to get more distance. I told him to hit it and run backwards."
- Ken Venturi, PGA golfer and US Open Champion, at a roast for columnist Art Rosenbaum

Here's proof that long term goals will enhance your performance on the golf course. One recent goal that I set for my golf game was to try to pass the PGA's playing ability test. It is the skill test that all PGA professionals must pass before they are eligible to enroll in the PGA training program. It is a one day, 36-hole test, sponsored by the PGA, and hosted at various courses throughout the spring, summer, and fall. The target score is typically between 151 and 156 depending on the course rating. If you can shoot back to back 77s or 78s, you will be on the bubble. The test is an unbelievable grind and typically, only five or six pass out of fifty or sixty players.

CONDITION

Actually, I have rarely shot back to back 77s and never in the same day. The test became a great challenge and motivated me to practice (something that I have never done because I just love to play). I've taken the test seven times this year and my handicap has dropped from a twelve to a seven. The first test was my introduction to the intensity of competitive golf. I was emotionally unprepared for the mental intimidation of playing 36 holes with almost no margin for error. I missed passing by 15 strokes. Test two I missed the target by 10 strokes. Test three and four missed the mark by three strokes (in the driving rain) and two strokes (in 100 degree heat). However, in my fourth attempt I shot one-under (my first round under par) and had my first hole-in-one on the first eighteen holes. I choked on the second eighteen with 6 three-putts, 2 balls OB, and cruised to an 84 to miss by two shots. Test five I prepared by not preparing and missed by 13. Test six I missed by 16 strokes on a windy, 35 degree day. Test seven I passed one day before this book went to print. I'm playing the best golf of my life because for the first time in 15 years I established a specific goal.

Before you play, have a target in mind for a score that you want to shoot. If you want to break 80, you have to shoot one over par every three holes. Another target can also be just to have fun. In that case, don't worry about where you're hitting the ball. Just go out and have a good time. That is the easiest target to hit and it may be the trick to bringing back your A-game.

"Take Dead Aim."
- Harvey Penick, PGA Golf instructor

In golf, as in business, having a target is critical, whether it is a goal for your round or a goal for the season. You will have more fun and feel a greater sense of satisfaction. Know what you are aiming for before every shot. Without a target, there is no way to measure your success.

3rd Tee ➡

Put on your hard hat for La Quinta Country Club's Mountain Course, par three, 16th. Palm Springs, California.

NUMBER 3 – WORK ETHIC

Work ethic is the toughest hole on this golf course. By a mile! Handicap Number 1. It's long, uphill, out of bounds to the right, water to the left, a small island green, and it always plays into the wind. No cart today, we're walking 36, with your heavy bag, and it's a hot one.

Prepare yourself not to be intimidated by hard work. On this hole we'll see why there is no such thing as easy money and why work is the best place you can go to ensure your success. I will show you that the last 5 percent of anything you do is the toughest, and that talk and action are on opposite sides of the performance chart. Get ready to improve your luck and recommit yourself to perseverance. Call home and tell them you'll be late, we've got a lot of work to do.

The single largest barrier to success is the soft work ethic. A good work ethic takes ideas to action, puts pen to paper, and picks up the telephone.

Hard work overcomes every other weakness. Most people fail because their work ethic stops half a turn short of where they really need to go. They do not ask that last question. They do not send that last thank-you note or return that last e-mail. It is the next level of pain at the finish line. Soft work habits are characteristics of the unsuccessful. The foundation for success is the willingness to work harder than the next person. Sweat equity is a reality. It is not only the extra hour in the office, it is also the willingness to stay that extra hour. Attention to detail and understanding the importance of the "little things" that make a big impact will enhance your work ethic.

Action cures fear. Taking action is one of the most satisfying things you can do and the only solution to every problem. Take a Saturday afternoon and go to the library and research an idea. You will be more satisfied than if you had sat on the couch and watched a golf tournament. Satisfaction from acting is a great source of pride.

There is no such thing as easy money. The only people that get rich quick are the lottery winners and the trust fund club. The rest of us have to earn it. Jumping from career to career is a great way to stay in second gear. It takes 18 months, minimum, to have an impact on any new endeavor. Find something that you want to do and stick with it. If you do change careers, pick one that you can stick with for at least five years. Grind it out and make it work before moving on to something new. Success does take time.

"Most golfers prepare for disaster. A good golfer prepares for success."
- Bob Toski, PGA Golfer

If you are starting a new business, you will be lucky if you make any money in the first three years. (My business squeaked by for the first three years. Year four we actually made a little money, not much, but a little something for the effort.)

It is almost impossible to describe how hard Charlie, my partner, and I worked while building our business. Our backgrounds included a fair amount of work just getting to that stage. I had a paper route when I was ten. I cut grass and washed cars for anyone that would hire me. I installed an air conditioner for a neighbor when I was 12. In high school, I lifeguarded, taught swimming lessons, washed dishes, and cleaned bathrooms and mopped floors at the YMCA. I worked full-time every other semester in college, painted dorms, sold cars, drove a forklift in a lumberyard, and just accepted it as a way of life. Charlie grew up with the same kind of great parents who expected him to earn his way from an early age as well.

*To build our business we went underground. We lived in fear, and life got serious for a few years. We worked until we passed out. Charlie worked harder than I did. What a horse. We **knew** it would pay off, and that it wasn't supposed to be easy. If you head butt the drywall long enough, you will break through.*

If you have children, teach them the importance of hard work. My parents had more to give, but by giving less I now have more. They knew what they were doing. Thanks, Mom and Dad! It's only fitting that I am finishing this sentence at 4:46a.m. When was the last time you were working at 4:46a.m.?

Every race is won by inches, and it is only won at the very end. The trouble is that too often we never know where the finish line is. I am referring to a sale, a project or an idea. The first 95 percent of anything is going to be done by everyone, but it's the last painful, and I mean painful, 5 percent that separates the winners from the losers. The trick is to deliver that last 5 percent with the same enthusiasm, positive attitude, and optimism that you had during the initial stages. It is during that last push, when the process can lose momentum, that the winners have the stamina to keep pushing.

"Don't get discouraged; it is often the last key in the bunch that opens the lock."
- Anonymous

Lawn mower or vacuum cleaner? You decide. The carpeted fairway of the 14th hole on PGA West's Stadium Course . Palm Springs, California.

If you have ever built a home, or had one built, the last 5 percent seems to take 50 percent of the time and effort. That is just a fact. That is also the difference between a 9 and an 8 handicap. Inches. Do not lose the 95 percent that you have done by not being brave enough to close it out with a bang. Inches!

Lucky people work hard. It is a correlation that always holds true. You know who they are right away.

Spend energy, not money, on new ideas. There's plenty of legwork that you can do to test any idea before you have to spend a dime. Turn over every stone yourself before paying someone else to turn them over for you. However, it means getting up off the couch. It takes courage to make a sacrifice. Get started and do not stop 'til you are done.

Go to work! It is where you spend no money but can make as much as you want. Try to stretch your normal workday by at least an hour. Stay focused during that hour, and you will double your normal production. That extra hour or so lets you start your next day with a plan.

Walk the walk. Ideas are great, but it is your responsibility to turn an idea into reality. We are all envious of the people trying to make something happen. Admit it. Watching someone chase a dream motivates the winners and is sour grapes to the rest of the world. Resistance to a new idea can be overwhelming. Let your work ethic enlighten the naysayers.

There are different places to expend your energy. Do as many favors as possible for as many people as you can. Develop a plan to work hard at getting to know as many people as possible. Socializing and making new friends is fun and can open doors that may have been inaccessible yesterday.

"Keep on going and the chances are that you will stumble on something, perhaps when you are least expecting it. I have never heard of anyone stumbling on something sitting down."
- Charles Kettering, General Motors President

Do not be afraid to ask for favors or for help. The H word is not your typical four-letter word. "Excuse me, could I ask you to do a favor for me?" is a request that is rarely denied. We want to say yes before we even hear the request. People inherently want to help other people. It creates a genuine bond.

Sometimes it is better to bring your door to opportunity than to wait for opportunity to come knocking. If you can only play one hole on my course, play this one. Twice.

How do you take your work ethic to the golf course? Trying to improve is the first whack at actually improving. For us weekend warriors the best thing you can do is take a series of lessons from an instructor. Most golf courses have a teaching pro. A series of lessons can touch all aspects of your game. If you can only work on one area, the short game will have the most impact on your score. Practicing your chipping, putting, and the game from inside 100 yards will lower your score the quickest.

If you are serious about golf, make an investment in a golf club. Golf clubs come in a variety of financial options; private clubs, semi-private clubs, or public courses where you can prepay for your rounds. There are plenty of clubs that offer unlimited golf privileges for a monthly fee. When you are not taking forty or fifty dollars out of your pocket to play each time, you will play more.

Joining a club offers the benefit of meeting people and making new friends. It will have an immense impact on your quality of life. Just drive to the course and ask for the membership director or head pro.

As a member of a golf club, I have been invited to play with groups of new friends in Palm Springs, Bermuda, Pinehurst, Sarasota, and Las Vegas. I have been a guest at Pine Valley, Robert Trent Jones, Congressional, and all of the courses pictured in this book. One fellow member included me in a fishing tournament in Venezuela where I landed 2 blue marlins and got hooked on sport fishing. I have met Michael Jordan, Dan Patrick of ESPN, college basketball coaches, and powerful businessmen and women. You won't become best friends with all of them, but you will be invited to places you can't get to on your own. Best of all, you will make some lasting friendships that begin with the common bond of being members of the same club.

If you want to play more golf, include your husband, wife, or significant other. It's a great way to combine the two things you love the most. Establish a set time each week or month when you and your friends will get together and play. If you can play more, you will improve.

THE WALL STREET JOURNAL

"I figure practice puts your brains in your muscles."
- Sam Snead, PGA Golfer

Get the ball to the hole. Most golf shots are short as opposed to long. Make sure you take enough club to get the ball past the hole. Especially putts and chips. If you have to hit a five iron from 150 yards out, hit it. Clubbing to someone else's distance is like ordering a meal that you don't like because the person next to you ordered it. Do not go through life short and hungry. Start your round hitting approach shots past the hole and then club down as necessary. Comeback putts are easier than second putts left short. You get a look at the break as it rolls past the hole.

Get a tee time. Call people that you would like to get to know better, and ask them to join you. I'm grateful when anyone, regardless of how little I know them, calls with a tee time looking for a fourth (or second for that matter). If there are business colleagues or friends that you'd like to get to know better, call them up and ask them to play. They will appreciate that you thought enough of them to ask. No one is invited to play golf too often.

Take a little bit of your work ethic out to the golf course. Tweak your flexibility routine before hitting the first tee. Any time you make a change in an effort to improve, you will achieve some degree of improvement.

"Big Shots are only little shots who keep shooting."
-Christopher Morley, Author

Club selection is key to your success on the cliffside, 16th hole of Gulf Harbour Golf Club. Hibiscus Coast, New Zealand.

NUMBER 4 - EQUIPMENT

When your only tool is a hammer, every problem begins to resemble a nail. Investing in the right equipment is often the difference between success and failure.

"The old one didn't float too well."
- Craig Stadler - PGA golfer, on being asked why he
was using a new putter at the 1992 US Open

On this hole, you will learn why the right equipment is important, and how equipment purchases influence your business and become a commitment to a process. I'll share the lowdown on service agreements (buying and selling), and when to purchase the low-cost alternative. You will also learn what the golf club manufacturers do not want you to know. Like a slow golf cart, the wrong equipment will add consistent frustration on your journey to success.

I realize that you may have nothing to do with how your company buys equipment, and if that is the case, use these equipment concepts to convince your cheap boss to buy you what you should have had in the first place. If you need new equipment to do your job better, use the following ideas to justify how your company will be more profitable if you have access to those assets. It's an easy sell. Scrutinize your work environment. The right tools, combined with the best techniques, are the keys to increasing productivity.

Cheap is expensive in disguise. The best philosophy for any business is to buy the best. Unfortunately, when spending money for business assets (or gripping a golf club), our natural tendency is to hold too tight. Loosen up and you will get better results with less pain. When it comes to the tools of your trade - cell phones, computers, heavy equipment, office furniture, technology investments, whatever - get the best and don't look back. You do get what you pay for, and it is a fact that we only regret paying too little.

Cheap companies buy cheap equipment. . . and then buy it again two years later.

My partner educated me about the importance of buying the best equipment very early in our business relationship. When we were just starting out he proposed purchasing the fastest, highest capacity, most powerful computers that were on the market. As my jaw was dropping he added "And we'll figure out a way to buy the best-looking furniture too. If we're going to be working with and looking at this stuff 20 hours a day, it's going to be top shelf!" Amen. His optimism of where we were headed and what type of company he wanted to build put another rivet in our partnership. All of the computers were in operation and the furniture still looked rich when the company was sold seven years later. High quality equipment will add pride to your organization and consequently increase productivity and morale. The latest and greatest may cost more, but it will last longer, give you fewer headaches, become obsolete on a slower schedule, and maintain its value.

Here is why your equipment purchases are critical: The wrong equipment will expose itself repeatedly, and in some cases, immediately. However, the right equipment will have almost no apparent impact on your business. You will not even know it is there. You will forget that it is actually doing a job. When computers were primarily used as word processors and generated more paper, our software company adopted a technique (before its time) that forced our employees to maximize the utilization of this technology. To guarantee an automated, paperless, environment we intentionally never bought a copier. All contracts, proposals, and documentation resided on our network and could be shared, e-mailed, faxed or scanned (before this was cool) without getting up or searching through files. Clients would have information electronically transferred to them before the phone call was over. We looked like champs, and before long, no one ever thought about a copier. If any area of your business is exposing itself as a hindrance, make some changes. A smooth-running operation feels effortless.

Payroll does not stop when equipment does. Downtime for employees is the most expensive overhead for any business. Factor this into your decisions, and what to buy becomes a little clearer.

You are what you buy. Looking for a new job? The new company's equipment, office space, and furniture are an indication of how they may treat you. Hiring? Look around, your equipment says a lot about you.

Do not forget about your rich Uncle Sam. Up to a certain limit, every business purchase is a tax-deductible investment so spend those pre-tax dollars. Uncle Sam is kicking in a nice subsidy. Spending pre-tax dollars is the equivalent of a discount coupon equal to your tax rate. In most cases, 25 to 50 percent.

The act of replacing or repairing equipment has no value to your business. It is also significantly more costly than just the obvious expenditure of the repair bill or new item. Costs associated with time to order, training, purchasing, installation and removal do not show up on an invoice, but they are there. Purchase equipment with longevity in mind.

"My old man's a TV repair man. He's got an ultimate set of tools. I can fix it."
- Sean Penn, as Jeff Spicoli in Fast Times at Ridgemont High

There are different purchasing criteria for different items. So how do you determine how much to spend on what? Two questions to ask before making any purchase are, "Will I still want this and will this still work five years from now?" If you cannot answer "yes," buy something else.

What do the millionaires do? Be careful to avoid confusing "luxury" items with good quality equipment. Expensive cars and clothes are luxury items and should be purchased using different criteria. America's millionaires are profiled in the best selling book, "The Millionaire Next Door", and surprisingly, 50 percent of all millionaires in this country have never paid more than $399 for a suit or more than $140 for a pair of shoes. If you don't have a "cool mil" in the bank, check your closets, we may know why.

Furniture should not be considered a "luxury" item - quality furniture is a necessity. When leasing office space, have nicer offices than your competitors. But not too much nicer! If nothing else, just furnish your office more elegantly.

Your car is the most important piece of equipment that you will own. As a business asset, a clean, reliable, automobile is all you really need. My first sales job was selling cars, so I have some inside information. Buy a used car in September or October. Dealerships are clearing their inventory at that time of year. A new car is a bad investment because it drops 10 percent to 25 percent in value on your drive home. Most automobile styles cycle every four or five years. Where you are on that cycle is very difficult to determine with the naked eye. All manufacturers will tell you when they are planning to change body styles. A $10 car wash will make your car look a year or two newer. There can be a significant difference, $10,000 or $20,000, between the cost of a new car versus the cost of the same clean, reliable car with the same body style that is a few years old. The difference in price has no value other than "personal satisfaction." Oh, and "The Millionaire Next Door" will also tell you that most millionaires buy used cars.

Do not try to make money with your car when it comes to taxes. Pick one method (mileage or a percentage of costs) for tax purposes and get on with it. The IRS has covered all the angles.

Recognize when you should purchase only the items with the absolute lowest cost. Examples include office supplies, long distance phone charges, dry-cleaning, gasoline, life insurance, bottled water, and mortgages. When borrowing money, if you can save a quarter of a point on the interest rate, why wouldn't you? One mortgage is no different from the next. When shopping for a mortgage, compare at least three, and tell each banker that you are only going to purchase the lowest rate. The one who keeps listening will be competitive. The ones who try to tell you why their mortgage is a better mortgage will not have the lowest rate. Most will not return your calls when they understand it is a rate race. Do not pay mortgage points if you can avoid it. Determine when price is the only evaluating factor and purchase accordingly.

When should you purchase a service or maintenance agreement? Buying a prepaid service agreement should be based on the importance of the item. If your business cannot survive without a specific item, a service agreement may be a good idea as an extra incentive to the service provider to put your service call at the top of the queue. Service agreements can be great, but only for the right products. Service agreements will typically offer a discount or better service terms than purchasing service after a malfunction. Some service agreements include scheduled maintenance; filter changes, belt changes, lubrication, etc. If you buy an appliance from Sears, their extended warranties include scheduled maintenance. Roger, the appliance salesperson, told me that very few customers take advantage of the maintenance portion of the agreement.

Never buy an unwarranted automobile without adding the cost of a service agreement. An automobile service agreement will cost you two thousand dollars or less. A steal for the peace of mind of free repairs for the next 50,000 miles. I have never owned a car that needed less than $2,000 worth of service in 50,000 miles. Free peace of mind? No brainer.

Short-term service agreements (coverage of less than a year) are not good investments. Stereos, televisions, and appliances come to mind. Work with the manufacturer or your supplier if you have equipment failure in the first year. Use credit cards when making purchases for an additional 30-day window to guarantee that you receive what you thought you bought. Credit card companies are loyal to the consumer, and, in most cases, will credit your account if you are unsatisfied. Getting cash back after a dispute is almost impossible. Also, before signing the deal, have the warranty, cancellation, and return policies **in hand, in writing**. If a company does not stand behind their products, find another supplier.

Buying service agreements can be good, but providing service agreements is great. If I were a builder, I would try to sell my customers a service agreement guaranteeing that the building would not fall down. If the building did fall down, I would have my crew on-site in less than 24 hours putting that building back together, get this, at no cost! That sounds like a great deal to the buyer of the building, but in reality, the odds of the building falling down are next to nothing, so any revenue that you generate is pure profit. Silly concept? No, it's insurance.

Why not be in the insurance business when you can? How much car insurance have you paid for, and how many accidents have you had? Oh, that would be none. The insurance folks don't give much back. Fires? I have never had one. I don't know anyone that has had one. Nevertheless, I can't wait to pay for fire insurance, year in and year out!

Prepaid service is a great way to increase revenue and customers love it. A service agreement is also another reason to stay in touch with your clients and, if your products don't require much service, a great way to add 10 percent to 30 percent to each sale. Our software company's pricing included a maintenance fee to fix problems if the software failed. Every customer bought it. It was our best source of revenue, and most clients renewed annually.

You may not have enough club to get to Bulle Rock's 13th green. Havre De Grace, Maryland.

Sure you're on the hook, but you're on the hook anyway if you stand behind your products. The true value of our business became the recurring maintenance income that grew each year.

Even if it is not a standard practice in your industry, try to offer a maintenance or service agreement. Blaze a path to customer satisfaction. It was an afterthought for us, and it was the best thing we ever did. Do not be afraid to be the first to try it. The insurance business is easy to get into if you are creative.

Finally, face the music and perform all of the suggested maintenance activities on your equipment. Keep all of your equipment clean. Clean equipment runs better. It does not cost anything to keep things clean, and it is a policy with no downside.

"At 15, we put down my bag to hunt for a ball, found the ball, lost the bag."
- Lee Trevino, professional golfer, at Royal Birkdale

To play golf you need clubs, balls, tees and a bag. A glove is overrated as long as you can keep your hands dry. I have not used a glove in 10 years and haven't let go of a club yet. A healthy attitude is to feel that you can pick up any set of clubs and shoot about the same score on any given day. Remove the equipment excuse. Your clubs do not top the ball, you do.

So how come the golf equipment manufacturers convince us that their latest and greatest is the change we really need? Because we are hacks who love the game so much we want to believe there really is a cure! I hate to break it to you, but there is no cure. Not with only an equipment change.

The major difference from one club to the next is the grip. It is the only part of the club that you touch, and if you put a new grip on an old club, and a new grip on a new club, guess what? Those clubs feel the same. If you are just starting, buy a set of clubs from the paper. Get an old set and have them re-gripped. A golf game cannot be purchased. "All pay and no play" is a bad reputation to have.

All that matters is what feels good to you. A club that is comfortable to your eye as you look down before you swing is the most important criteria. You may prefer a heavier club. Steel shafts or graphite? Regular flex or stiff? Personal preference is all that matters.

Consistency is critical in your bag. Having the same type of shafts in all of your clubs will offer consistent results and feedback. It will also reduce any weight difference from one club to the next and increase your ability to repeat good swings. Have a full set of matching clubheads from one manufacturer. Removing any variance from your clubs will remove any mental second-guessing.

Keep your clubs clean. Have a wet towel and wipe off your clubs after each shot. You will feel a little better about hitting a clean club, and they will last longer.

Give your old clubs away. All golf clubs belong in someone's bag. Give them to a friend that wants to take up the game or to any junior golf program. The golf gods will not miss this act of generosity.

"You can buy a country, but you can't buy a golf swing. It's not on the shelf!"
-Gene Sarazen, professional golfer, to Henry Ford II

Putters can get in your head, but when you get down to it, putters are **all** a flat surface attached to the end of a stick. Brad Faxon, one of the PGA tour's best putters, says that "Confidence is the most critical element when putting and that if you do not care if the putt goes in, it will free your mind to make more putts." He did not say anything about the putter. Pick a putter that you like and stick with it. Some days they'll go in and some days they won't. It's never the putter's fault!

Buy your golf balls in bulk. Not just by the dozen, but by the case. Buying them a sleeve at a time will not keep you from losing them by the dozen. I also suggest you have your business logo on your golf balls. They become tax deductible and are great gifts for clients. That last errant shot may connect you with your next client.

Re-grip your clubs when they have the slightest slickness or wear. Always have a clean, new, good-looking bag. That is all anybody is going to see until you get to the first tee. After that, you are on your own.

After following these guidelines, fight the urge to buy new clubs when the game leaves you. And it will. Clubs do not lose distance or accuracy over time, it just seems that way. The objective is to get comfortable with the clubs you play with. Do not be the kind of golfer who blames his poor game on his equipment. Do you blame the telephone when you lose a sale?

5th Tee ➡

Austin Country Club's attractive Par 3, 2nd Hole. Austin, Texas.

NUMBER 5 - DRESS FOR SUCCESS

"Nice hat. Do you get a free bowl of soup with this?...Oh, but it looks good on you!"
- Rodney Dangerfield as Al Cervik, in Caddyshack

Get your camera ready; this hole is postcard perfect. Majestic pine trees shape this dogleg with an engineer's precision and line each side of the fairway like soldiers protecting the woods from its beauty.

The grass is groomed into perfectly alternating light and dark green diamonds fit for a chess game of the gods. You are absorbed by the perfection of the image and are oblivious to the trance engulfing you. Long shadows cool the right side of the fairway, and you are reminded why this is your favorite time of day to play. Three deer nonchalantly graze at the tree line and have no problem with you playing through. The elevated tee feels like a worn museum bench. Perfectly manicured rough becomes the dark green matting separating the pine straw frame from the art that is hole number 5. The power of time, the perfect balance of nature, and how great it is to be alive are thoughts that push you out of your trance and into your pocket for your ball and tee. A thousand words are not enough.

What impression did you make on the world today?

Don't brush off this chapter because you think you belong on the cover of GQ. Nobody stands in front of the mirror and admires how bad they look. Dressing for success encompasses more than your wardrobe. On this hole, you will learn that how you present yourself is a sign of where you want to be in life. I will share with you the one accessory that matches everything in your closet and the only thing that everyone remembers. You will see the value of organization and learn how to never lose anything ever again. In addition, if you have never stepped foot in a private Country Club, I will prepare you for your debut. Let's let it rip.

Organization is the preliminary step to dressing for success. Do you misplace things? Car keys? Files? If so, you have an organization problem. Losing or forgetting things is not an indication of a lack of intelligence, but a lack of organization. Organization is a great way to hide a failing memory. This chapter will help you organize all phases of your life.

When you are looking for something and you find it in the fourth place you look, move it to the first place that you looked when you put it back. When that item is not on your mind, this is where your brain tells you to go first. Do not fight your brain because it is a losing battle. Put things back so you can find them in the first place you search.

This technique is great for organizing computer files. Copy files into the directory or folder where you looked first. You can do a lot worse than having a couple of copies of the same file. Disk space is cheap. Add a backup directory for important files that may be accidentally erased. This has saved me more than once. Even Bill Gates has erased files by mistake. Invest some time organizing your computer files so you can get to the files you want immediately.

Computer reliability has improved, but it is still not bulletproof. Copy important files to removable disks just in case. If these files are larger than a diskette or two, I strongly recommend that you have a daily backup routine to some external removable device like a zip drive or tape backup drive. Keeping these removable backups in multiple locations can also be a lifesaver in case of theft, flood, or fire. Pretend that your computer is stolen every night and backup accordingly. I am not willing to lose one minute worth of work so I backup my files daily.

Neatness will add value to your life. Most of the people who are the best dressed at functions, the best dressed on the golf course, and the best dressed at work, also seem to be the most organized. There is a correlation, and one may drive the other. Disorganized people wear wrinkled clothes.

If you do not have a clean desk policy, invoke one now. Work on one activity at a time and clean off your desk at the end of every workday.

Smile. The easiest, least expensive, and most impressionable addition to your wardrobe is your smile. We spend incredible amounts of money on clothes to feel good about ourselves and to impress the world and the opposite sex. However, we forget about the value of a smile. Nothing will leave a more positive impression than a genuine smile. Before you buy your next suit, take the

Few holes dress up as well as Cattail Creek's signature 11th on a perfect fall day. Glenwood, Maryland.

money and visit your dentist. Let your dentist decide how to invest that money to improve your smile. You can whiten your teeth, have them cleaned, capped, flossed, or buffed, but get them in shape to be proud to show them off. That is your dentist's job, by the way. Any inhibitor that keeps you from flashing a great smile should be eliminated. Your smile is the suit you wear every day. Your face has to have some expression, so why not choose the most productive and pleasant one. Keep your smile as part of your daily wardrobe.

"The victim that smiles steals something from the thief."
-William Shakespeare, playwright

Your actual dress in the office is important. It is the most vital ingredient of your first impression. If you are presentable, neat, and dressed well, you are going to make a positive first impression. You may open your mouth and blow it, but at least give yourself a chance.

Make sure your clothes fit well. It is important to be comfortable. If clothes are too tight, or do not fit well, you will lose confidence.

Do not wear clothes that make you sweat. Basketball coaches can sweat through their clothes but you cannot. How much you sweat is linked to your physical fitness.

Exercise. If you are suffering from excessive perspiration or cannot get into your favorite duds, do yourself a big favor and get in shape. You will sweat less, your clothes will fit better, and you will look better. Organize your week to include at least three activities that will tax you physically. A good workout will jump-start your body and give you a sense of accomplishment to build upon. Clothes can only do so much with your frame, and your body shape dictates your overall appearance. A personal physical fitness plan is as big a part of your presentation to the world as your hygiene. Getting in shape is part of the preparation for success. Add physical fitness to your week, your day, your diet, and goals for success.

"Looking good and dressing well is a necessity. Having a purpose in life is not."
- Oscar Wilde, poet, playwright

Dress for the position you want. If you want that promotion, you may want to dress like your boss, or your boss's boss. You will never be thought of less for being well-dressed. Care about your appearance and how you are presented to the rest of the world.

I was introduced into corporate America and the influence of dressing for your desired position during my first internship with IBM. I worked in one of their manufacturing facilities and rotated through a variety of engineering departments. The majority of the engineers dressed well but the manufacturing environment, unlike the rest of IBM, had a relaxed dress code. After a few months in the engineering ranks it was clear to me that I would be happier in a sales or marketing position. I began wearing pressed shirts, suits, and ties. Basically, what the IBM sales force was wearing. In less than a few weeks my co-workers started teasing me about dressing like a salesman. A week or two later they actually suggested that my personality may have been better suited for a marketing position. My boss even helped me transfer into a marketing division for my next intern assignment. It was the start of a great career. Changing my dress was the first step and a subtle transition into the position that I sought. My first job after graduating from college was as an IBM sales representative.

Being neat and dressing well does not mean paying a lot of money. You can actually look good in a very inexpensive suit if you have a clean tie, pressed shirt, and shined shoes.

If your clients or constituents typically wear suits, I suggest you wear a suit every day. Even if you work in a dress-down environment, I do not think you can lose points by wearing a suit. You will feel more prepared to conduct business and probably do your job better. If your industry does not require a suit, coordinate your wardrobe to be the best-dressed for your industry's style. If you dress sharper than your coworkers, management will feel better about exposing you to new projects. Polishing your appearance will have a significant positive impact on your career and you will certainly be prepared for that unexpected meeting with your vice president. There is no down side to dressing like a pro. You never know where you're going to meet your next client, find your next business opportunity, or be placed in a position where you wish you were dressed to impress.

Keep your car clean. Inside and out. Asking clients or friends to "look out for the beer bottles" sends a parade of bad messages. Car washes are standard maintenance and tax deductible if your car is used for business purposes. If something on your car does not work, fix it immediately. How much your car costs is far less important than how well you take care of it.

A windbreaker is a good idea on Balybunion's seaside 11th. Balybunion, Ireland. (Photo. J. Tillery)

Exchange business cards with everyone you meet. "I left my cards at home" is an unacceptable statement. Make contacting you as easy as possible for new acquaintances by always carrying business cards. Have them in your car, your wallet or purse, in your briefcase, and in your golf bag. When collecting business cards, have one box where you keep them. Write notes on the back; how you met, mutual friends, and what they look like. Having notes on the back is the most important component. I was introduced to a sports photographer three years ago and tracked him down for help with this book. Without my card system I would have missed out.

How you dress may influence how you play on the golf course. Keep the plaid and neon in the closet. Strive to be the best-dressed in your foursome. If you can't play, you can at least look the part! From the parking lot to the first tee, let people think you've got game. "He looks good, but he can't play!" is better than just "He can't play!" Give yourself something.

If you play golf, at some point you will be invited to a country club. Don't worry, they don't bite. Country clubs are the ultimate in luxury, but club etiquette is an acquired skill. Here goes.

Country clubs treat members' guests very well. Do not be afraid to ask for anything, and do not be intimidated. Change your shoes in the locker room, not in the parking lot. Most clubs have a shoe attendant who will store your walking shoes while you play. They will be mysteriously shined when you return. Some clubs require long pants. Confirm that shorts are allowed before showing up. If it's not too hot, wear long pants; dressing like a pro may make you feel like one. Be prepared to tip the bag handlers and the locker room attendant (commonly referred to as "the shoe man"). Two to five dollars is fine. A one dollar tip is a little cheap. Get to know the shoe man's first name. You will see him more than any other club employee, and he is your butler for the day. Most have a great sense of humor and can guide you around the club if your host is not around. In addition, some clubs have a no tip policy. The staff will let you know if that is the case when you offer, and they will not be offended.

Some clubs require a coat and tie (most do not), but it does not hurt to ask. Most clubs have great locker room facilities. Cleaning up in a club locker room after your round will make you want to live there. Bring a change of clothes for the experience. Khakis and golf shirts are the typical country club dress code. Do not wear jeans or T-shirts at any time.

"Caddies are a breed of their own. If you shoot a 66, they say, 'Man, we shot 66!' But shoot 77, and they say, 'Hell, he shot 77!'"
- Lee Trevino, professional golfer

Caddies may be part of the country club experience. If you have not played golf with a caddy, you should. Not all courses offer caddy services. If they are an option, ask the member if you can play with a caddy. I am sure he or she will not object. Caddies charge $20 to $40 per bag, plus tip. Be prepared to pay $60 to $100 if they carry two bags. A caddy's round is called a loop. As a guest, pick up the caddy fee for yourself and the member. Do not be afraid of the caddy either. Caddies tell great stories and good jokes. They'll read putts (better than you will), clean your clubs, find your errant shots, rake traps, and make you feel like a pro. It's a great time.

As a guest in a club, privately offer to pay cash for drinks, food, and green fees. Most clubs do not take cash. Do not assume the member will pick up the tab. All clubs charge guest green fees. Drinks and dinner may appear to be free but they are not. Reimburse the member for the privilege of playing the course.

As a club member, all I care is that my guests offer to pay. I will usually pick up the tab. If you do not **offer** to pay, you have burned your return ticket. Golf, caddies, dinner, and drinks can get a little steep, so ask the member what the guest fees are beforehand.

Remember that the member has paid an initiation fee and monthly dues, so whatever the guest fee, you are getting a great deal. Send the member a thank you note and you will always be welcome back. Introduce yourself to the head pro, get one of his or her cards, and send a thank you note. You may want to go back and it never hurts to have the head pro remember you.

Go to the golf course and the office with the belief that you are going to meet somebody new and dress accordingly.

, Inc. All Rig *"I like the way my wallet feels in them."* **WALL STREET JOURNAL.**   *** * *

- Johnny Miller, when asked if he

n

n profit **Page B4.**   *liked the line of clothes he endorses*

6th Tee ➡

The ocean view is reason enough to leave the clubs in the trunk and settle into an afternoon of lawn bowling. Camps Bay, South Africa.

NUMBER 6 – FLEXIBILTY

Flexibility is a prerequisite for massive growth. Having the ability to bend without breaking and to be adjustable to change will introduce options that are not available to the rigid personalities of the world. This hole plays downhill, has gently flowing streams, and a light breeze always at your back. Loosen up and I will show you how to handle the negative influences in your life and teach you the power of **Yes**. We'll stretch the workday and learn how to retain the best ideas. We will get in touch with the world as a fluid, gentle river that we can float with or swim against. I will show you what to do five minutes before your tee time to enhance the next four hours, and how your attitude can turn your life into a permanent vacation.

"Happy is the man who can endure the highest and lowest fortune. He who can endure both with equal temperament has deprived misfortune of its power."
- Seneca, Roman philosopher

There are two types of flexibility. Physical flexibility and mental flexibility.

Physical flexibility refers to our body's ability to adapt to change, either gradual or sudden. The flexible athlete (and we are all athletic creatures) sustains fewer injuries and heals from those injuries more quickly. Physical flexibility can be achieved through exercise, stretching, and diet, and is a gradual development process that I recommend to everyone.

The power of <u>Yes</u>. Mental flexibility is easier to achieve than physical flexibility and can put the power of the masses in your hands. You can increase your mental flexibility by the end of this paragraph by incorporating a single thought into your mental vocabulary. That thought is **Yes**. The rigid mind thinks **No**. **No** that's not a good idea. **No** I don't like that. **No**, it should be done this way. **No**, I do not like them. **No**, we can't.

<u>No</u> is hard while <u>Yes</u> is easy.

Yes allows the light in. **Yes** opens the door and empowers the people. **Yes** turns a group into a team. **Yes** makes you laugh and smile. **No** makes you frown and justify. **No** is the start of a small battle and takes significantly more energy than **Yes**. **Yes** lets your brain breathe while **No** holds your mental breath. *Si, Como No?* is Spanish for Sure, Why Not? A little *Si, Como No* is great medicine to induce your mental flexibility.

Forget your ego. One way to be flexible at work is to forget your ego and pretend from time to time that you are not the local expert on every subject. I know it's hard, but try to actually learn something from everybody. The people of the world are dying to share their secrets, but not enough people are listening.

Always be open-minded, and listen to everyone's suggestions. A good idea is a good idea no matter who or where it comes from. I have seen too many good ideas taken off an agenda just because someone's ego got in the way. Evaluate each idea on its own merits, and pretend that the idea or suggestion was yours.

The objective is to recognize and act upon the good ideas, not come up with all of them.

"Egotism is the anesthetic which nature gives us to deaden the pain of being a fool."
- Anonymous

My wife and I had the opportunity to take a 6-week journey around the world (as evidenced by some of the photography in this book), and we were exposed to wonderful people all over the world. My basic belief has always been that people are people no matter where you are, so how did we tap into this generous, helpful, happy spirit in every country we visited? You may have encountered similar experiences in your travels. We concluded that how we approach other people is the key to the experience, and we can control most of that. Our attitude significantly influences the experience. An outstretched hand and a smile are usually reciprocated. Upon returning to the States, I continued treating everyone as if I were a visitor in their country. I asked questions about their families, their favorite pastimes or sports, and their hobbies and favorite foods. Basic questions we normally do not care to ask. The heavens opened, and the genuine spirit we saw around the world was here as well. We see a reflection of what we are offering. If you want to be on vacation for the rest of your life, tap into the spirit that surrounds you. The people of the world possess the qualities you are looking for - approach every level of humankind with warmth and a genuine interest, and you will be rewarded with a new appreciation of the human spirit.

Stay loose over your shot into the par 4, 6th hole of Joondalup Country Club. Perth, Western Australia.

Work longer. Be flexible enough to work longer hours. Get there earlier or stay later, but burn the midnight oil when the in-basket is a little heavier than normal. The nine-to-fiver is on the endangered species list and the "Save-The-Nine-to-Fiver" campaign never got off the ground because everyone left at five. Evolution has its advantages. Revolving your day around the five o'clock bell limits your ability to be productive and puts you in the inflexible category.

Karma. The cosmic world definitely has a rhythm and wave element that is just outside of our perception. The cycles of the tides and moon phases, the consistency of the seasonal changes, and the karma of the soul are all very real elements of our lives. Try to be in the sweet spot of those waves by saying **yes** more often. Accept the mistakes of others as mistakes and not the end of the world. Absorb the positive energy, and ignore the negative energy. I am a firm believer in seeking the groove in life. You may see this as pure fiction, but I have tapped into this wave and it is part magic and part connection with the human spirit, but it works. Being flexible is part of it. Let your mind believe that how you interact with the rest of the world can influence your position on the wave. Do not swim upstream.

MARKETPLACE

"Most of us don't recognize opportunity until we see it working for a competitor."
- Anonymous

If you always do what you always did, you will always get what you always got. A good test of your flexibility is how you have evaluated yourself against the concepts of this book. If your first thoughts as you read were, sure I do that, I do that too... Maybe you just want to solidify your lofty status. If you are testing yourself and challenging yourself as you read, you have developed some degree of mental flexibility. Flexibility is a requirement for change.

Be prepared to deal with the unpleasant people of the world. They are dishonest, mean, petty, and obnoxious (to put it nicely). In addition, they have to live and work somewhere, so be ready. Start by being nice to them, today. Look for any positive quality they may have, and open your mind to their suggestions. If you can do this, you can be in complete control of all of your relationships. Know that they will always be a stone in your shoe, but let your patience expose their limitations. Be nice, be fair, and let the problem lie with them, not you. Leaders possess this type of flexibility.

Be flexible to accommodate unique situations. In business, unique situations are part of the scenery. If every situation were a rubber stamp, business would be easy. Employees would not steal, customers would prepay for everything, and you would hug your banker. Have your mind prepared to handle these curve balls as they present themselves. Being open-minded to the exceptions is a display of wisdom. Flexibility is listening to customers. When customers tell us what they want, deliver exactly what they ask for as opposed to what you are selling.

This foursome of Waterbuck are simply waiting on the threesome of impala who have been holding them up all day. Elephant Hills Golf Club. Victoria Falls, Zimbabwe.

Position your business to be flexible, to be able to move with what the customer needs. Keep your mind open to all ideas. Take your ego out of the equation or it will cost you cash. Flexibility with others is a form of generosity. You cannot be too flexible or too generous.

If there is a fountain of youth, I'm sure it serves Bud, Bud Light, and Flexibility on tap. Stay loose. As we age, we gradually lose flexibility. Old people get stiff. Stay flexible and you will stay young.

Maintaining flexibility on the golf course is critical to your success. This includes physical flexibility as much as mental flexibility. Golf can wreak havoc on your body. Stretching jump starts your body's musculoskeletal system and reduces injuries.

Stretch. You certainly feel better on the first tee after stretching. While you are stretching, find a positive state of mind and visualize your goals for the day. Nothing too crazy here; a five-minute stretching routine is plenty. Sit down and stretch your back, your shoulders, and the backs of your legs. Stretch your fingers and loosen your wrists. Keeping your wrists loose is a great way to let the club head and the swing take care of itself. Without stretching, your muscles are gradually going to loosen up as you play. If you stretch beforehand, you will reduce how much your body and your swing change during your round. A five-minute stretching routine is better than hitting balls or putts. Get your body and mind in sync.

Drink plenty of water. The body is mostly water. The more water you have in your system the more efficiently it will work. My experience has been that I think better, feel better, and play better after drinking a quart of water. Do not wait until you are thirsty to replenish your body with its main ingredient. Drink plenty of water to maintain your fluidity.

As you are now aware, flexibility starts in the mind. Be flexible with who you will play with. Unfortunately, golf has a tendency to be a little-rich-kid's sport, which is what I like least about the game. Be flexible enough to play with anyone, and keep your attitude positive. Some golfers do not like to play with golfers that are not of their caliber. Enjoy your round with all levels of golfers, and do not get caught in the trap of playing with the same three people every Saturday.

> *"A wise man doesn't just wait for the right opportunity. He creates the right opportunity. Do not wait for ideal circumstances or for the best opportunities. They will never come."*
> *- Ben Franklin, American Statesman*

Be flexible to the outside influences that can distract you. If somebody accidentally drops a club in your backswing, big deal. If somebody walks in your line, no sweat. I have never missed a putt because of a spike mark or somebody's footprint. (I figure that's over 20,000 putts.)

Use your pre-round stretching routine to relax your mind. Remind yourself that you are playing golf, not working. Set the goals for the day, and go out and achieve them. Be flexible to the outside influences, and enjoy your round of golf, regardless of who you are playing with, their pace of play, or their skill level.

7th Tee ➡

Don't let your golf ball's splash interrupt the serenity surrounding Golden Horseshoe's 16th green. Williamsburg, Virginia.

NUMBER 7 - CALM

Want to be respected? Stay calm, cool, and collected.

On the tee of this hole it is so quiet you can hear yourself breathe. The lake is a perfect reflecting mirror, and the leaves are snapshot-still. The world seems to have stopped dead in time. The temperature is so perfect it goes unnoticed. You are not cool or warm. You are standing in the shade, and the sun is behind you. You are not squinting, and the colors are as bright as they will ever be. You see rich, green grass, and a gold flag in the distance. It is almost surreal. Capturing peace and tranquillity is the purpose of this hole. At times like these the power of all of your senses becomes magnified. Hence, the power of calm. When wind, rain, hunger, thirst, blistering heat, or brittle cold do not stress your body, the senses are freed from their normal distractions and can operate at peak performance.

"Adopt the pace of nature, her secret is patience."
-Ralph Waldo Emerson, American Author and Philosopher

This hole will teach you the secrets of reducing stress in your daily affairs, and show you how it will add years to your life. You will see that a calm mind will enhance your creativity and introduce clarity. You will also learn that a calm mind is a great defensive position that will gracefully get you out of difficult situations in life and on the golf course. Stay calm as we glide through this hole, and you will see that remaining calm is all upside and a prerequisite to being the go-to person in any situation.

Remaining calm is the most rational state of mind. The best visibility on the open seas occurs during the calmest weather. This holds for your vision as well. To visualize and act clearly, put emotion aside and evaluate stressful situations as if they were happening to someone else. This will introduce a new level of objectivity and help you organize your thoughts.

All great leaders possess the ability to stay calm. The more severe the pressure or problem, the greater benefit a calm disposition offers. When serious issues present themselves, stay calm to focus on the solution. Here are some ideas that should help you keep your emotions in check.

No matter what happens, the sun is going to rise tomorrow. The best business advice I ever received was, "Don't let the highs be too high or the lows be too low!" Getting from upset to calm is a real trick. When frustration or anger finds you, put the phone down, stop and take a few deep breaths and exhale slowly. Take a slow walk for a minute or two with the objective being to let the steam out of your system. Force your face to make a smile. While you are smiling repeat to yourself that you will control this, it will not control you. Now go back to your desk and calmly design your action plan. On paper. Once things get written down they become less intimidating. "This, too, shall pass."

The only thing you can completely control is how you react to the craziness that can find you on any given day. It is how situations are handled that are lasting memories, not the situations themselves. A crisis can actually be an opportunity to display your leadership qualities and show others that you can be cool in the fire.

Customers, bosses, friends, and business associates will at one point or another be disappointed, neglected, or just plain angry for no reason, and the blame will somehow swim into your lagoon. Sometimes you are the reason and sometimes you are not, but at this stage it does not matter. You have found yourself at the center of the crisis, and the calmer your disposition, the more beneficial you can be to the situation.

During the negotiations for the sale of my business, calm became my secret weapon. Calm is huge in negotiations. Buyers typically have all of the leverage. Sellers can help themselves to better terms or a better price by exuding a sense of calm.

In my case, various incidences happened through the course of negotiations that could have soured the deal. One situation occurred when one of my employees handed me a letter he found slipped under our office front door. The letter was a formal offer to purchase my business. It was not in an envelope, just the letter. My staff had no idea that I was even thinking about selling the company. Until that moment, anyway. It was around 4:30 p.m. and people got scarce around 5, so I had about

*15 minutes to get my thoughts together if I wanted to address the situation before everyone left. Thought one - the employee who found the letter did not read the bold **Subject: Offer to Purchase Corporation**. Thought two - forget about thought one, no one could have missed it. Thought three - the truth is never that bad so I quickly evaluated the pros and cons and decided that the staff would need to know at some point. I called a quick meeting before everyone left for the day and said a buyer was making an offer for the business and it was too early in the process to even consider it a possible option. I reminded everyone their jobs were safe, and I would keep them posted if developments progressed. I openly stated I wanted to avoid any rumors, and they could ask me any questions at any time. A few questions floated up, but none of the staff seemed too concerned. They saw it as business as usual.*

The letter being left at the door could have been an honest mistake. It also could have been a negotiating ploy to force the cat out of the bag in my office. My next move was to use this to my advantage in our negotiations. I called the buyer and calmly let him know that I had received his formal offer and two things became apparent. One, the offer was too low and the terms for payment did not meet my requirements and two, the sloppiness of his business practices was a new concern because the success of my business was very important to me. He apologized and said he would get back to me. I stayed calm and assumed the deal was off. Three weeks went by and I was sure the deal was dead. I bumped into his accountant and he asked how the deal was going. I told him my counter offer must have been too rich. I even followed that up with a "but the business is doing so well, it is probably best that I stay the course. Tell him thanks anyway." The accountant said he would have the buyer call me. When I got back to my office the phone was ringing. It was the buyer. He said he would like to buy the business under the terms of my counter offer. The deal was put together. Staying calm allowed me to minimize the buyer's leverage. If I had appeared too eager to sell, too eager to forgive the sloppiness of the letter incident, or too eager to wait for his call, I would have sold the business, but for his number instead of mine. Calm is quiet strength.

Ask questions. If you ever watched the television show "Colombo" you understand the value of calm questioning. I know it was only TV, but his continuous questioning always kept him calmly in control of the situation. Bring that detective technique into all of your explosive situations. Ask plenty of questions with no targets in mind. Who is at fault is incidental. Keep a sense of humor about you. Make a joke or humorous gesture to establish the peace. Calmly looking for short and long term solutions will establish you as the clutch performer when problems arise. People will equate you with having a level head. If you are the head of a group, listen calmly to as many people as possible before speaking or acting. This lets you table the situation with the most information.

Buy time. Time allowed in any situation results in better decisions. It blows my mind how often people rush to action before they actually have to. Additional time will help you line up your options and make the best decision, with the least confusion in the shortest time. Respond to real deadlines not imaginary ones.

"On the whole it is patience which makes the final difference between those who succeed or fail in all things. All the greatest people have it in an infinite degree, and among the less, the patient weak ones always conquer the impatient strong."
- John Ruskin, American writer and art critic

Never threaten anyone or raise your voice. Nobody wants to work with a hothead. There is very little upside to raising your voice. People work more efficiently when they know that if they make a mistake they will not get screamed at. It is a sign of respect.

Calm

Don't fight. Negotiate. Calm leaders fight only as a last resort. Battles can be dangerous. Sometimes it is best to just lay low, keep your opinions to yourself, and not create any enemies. Only fight battles for reasons. If you do not have a good reason, do not fight the battle. You can put yourself in the loss column when you do not have to play the game. Pick your battles and evaluate your upside before you do anything.

Remaining calm reduces negative consequences. Some situations may appear to have a positive purpose but actually have only "downside." Having the last word, temper tantrums, being rude to someone who is rude to you, flipping off someone in traffic, and foul language are all actions that have only downside. However, we have to fight the urge to keep from doing them all. You may be fool enough to think that "getting something off your chest" will somehow advance your interests. It doesn't. It is all downside. Most arguments have no upside. What do you gain by winning an argument? You actually may gain an enemy. Stay calm and you will never have to apologize.

Stay calm to avoid stress. I believe that stress is the worst toxin you can have in your body. It is an invisible killer. We often hide stress or become oblivious to it. Physicians at Harvard Medical School have linked stress to a variety of health ailments including psychological problems, an increase of susceptibility to diseases, digestive troubles, weight problems, sleep disturbances, sexual and reproductive dysfunction, and a loss of concentration. One study suggested that stress is responsible for an increased incidence of death in a spouse whose partner has died within the previous six months. Incidents of acute stress often precede sudden heart-related deaths. During the 1996 Los Angeles earthquake a significant increase in sudden cardiac death occurred. Only a few of the deaths were related to physical exertion. Calm is not found in the medical journals introducing any pathological effects.

Extended periods of calm will unlock your creative powers. New ideas and clever thoughts just float to the surface of your consciousness when your mind is relaxed. If you have not created a new thought or idea in a while, revisit your level of calm. Try to pay your bills early, exercise a bit more, drink one cup of coffee instead of three, and get plenty of rest. Waking up without an alarm is a calm way to begin the day.

Trying to stay calm on the course can be a golfer's biggest challenge. "Relax, you can't play bad golf forever" is what you should remind yourself when you lose your cool. Just about every round has some period where you absolutely lose your mind. With this in mind, be prepared for a little "what the heck happened there?"

"In terms of its influence on the golf swing, the pre-shot routine is underestimated - hugely so in my opinion."
- Ernie Els, professional golfer

Golf pros say, "You can't win a tournament on Friday, but you can certainly lose it on Friday." Take a little bit of that mentality into your golf rounds. You cannot have a great round on the first hole, but you can certainly ruin a great round on the first hole.

Be patient. If you botch a hole or two early in the round, don't let it take you into a negative frame of mind. Eighteen holes gives you plenty of time to make up for mistakes on the first five or six holes. You can still have that career round if some things turn around.

Do not throw a temper tantrum and ruin someone else's day. They paid their green fees just like you. The club toss event is still not an Olympic sport so there's no need to practice.

CONDITION

You cannot be calm on the golf course when you need to be at work. You'll be halfhearted at two things that day. Golf responsibly, and know when to say when.

Concentrate, but don't try too hard. Losing your cool, in some cases, comes from trying too hard. We're so anxious to hit our next shot (to finally hit a good one after a small string of bad ones), that our anxiety level takes us farther from our normal game, normal rhythm, or swing. Playing with someone you want to impress or someone you want to beat badly can significantly alter your disposition. Tournament conditions and certainly gambling conditions also add to the intensity. "Out-calming" your opponents is one step closer to "you-da-man."

Stay in the present. Once you hit a shot, good or bad, it's over. You cannot take it back. The next shot is where your mental energy should be directed.

Slow down over the ball. You do not have a train to catch. Rush to your ball but don't rush your shot. Try not to hit out of turn, and take a little extra time over the ball. Implement a pre-shot routine that includes a mental thought to remain calm. Be aware of your state of stress. Golf can make us act like a baby like no other sport. Bad lies and bad breaks seem to strike at the worst time. Fight the tendency to whine about your game. You da man and da man don't whine.

To get the most enjoyment out of the game, smile and laugh as much as possible - especially after a poor shot. Forget about the last bad shot or hole and remember the 10-footer for par you made on hole number two. Block out any negative influences that may be on your mind outside of the golf course - personal relationships, work, etc. Loosen your grip to make sure your wrists are relaxed and agile. Jack Nicklaus suggests keeping your lower jaw relaxed to relax your entire upper body.

Remaining calm can be a challenge. Be aware of your stress level and it is easy to control.

8th Tee ➡

Calm

It's easy to get comfortable as another perfect sunrise awakens the beautiful 17th of La Quinta's Dunes course. Palms Springs, California.

NUMBER 8 - COMFORT ZONE

Wouldn't it be great if everything was easy? Understanding your comfort zone is your ticket to Easy Street. The comfort zone improvement concept is the gradual changing of habits so that you accomplish more while putting forth the same effort. Your comfort zone is your personal cruise control on the road to success.

This hole is shaped perfectly for your game. Here you will learn that maximizing your comfort zone is similar to getting more distance while using less effort in your golf swing. It can also be applied to any area of your life. Get comfortable with me as I offer six tips to improve your results-to-effort ratio. Par this hole and you will begin to visualize your personal improvement as a gradual fine-tuning of your activities. The proper use of the comfort zone technique will also bring a new level of confidence and performance on the golf course.

Whether you wear a Rolex or a Timex, all you get is 24 hours. If we all have the same 24 hours, why do some people accomplish more than others? Changing your comfort zone is your upgrade to a Rolex.

What is your comfort zone? Your comfort zone in your career is what you are comfortably able to produce in a week, a month, or a year. How can you break through your comfort zone? How do you chart your current comfort zone? Begin by placing a dollar value on all of your activities. Not your dollars, but the dollars of value that you generate based on the activities that you do.

Be deliberate. Scrutinize your actions throughout the day to determine if those actions increase the value of the dollars you generate. Remember that this is a **gradual** change of habits. It may be as simple as reorganizing when you do certain activities. I rearranged my day so that I arrived at work and left from work to avoid the congestion of traffic. That small change gave me an extra 30 minutes each day to be productive. That's an extra two days each month.

Maximize your results-to-effort ratio. Your results-to-effort ratio ensures that you perform the activities that have the highest level of productivity or return on investment. Evaluating your results-to-effort ratio forces you to only work on activities that accomplish your goals. Remember that time is the enemy and maximizing your output is your objective. Stop activities that do not accomplish your goals.

"No one would have crossed the ocean if they could have gotten off the ship in the storm."
- Charles Kettering, General Motors President

Tip #1. Monitor the time that you are productive. Limit your personal business to thirty minutes, during a specific time during the day, possibly after lunch. Do not waste time talking to friends, or handling personal business sporadically throughout the day. If you track the amount of time you spend on personal business, you may find you waste quite a bit. You will get your job done, but you will not improve your comfort zone.

Tip #2. Learn new skills. Invest time in training yourself, your staff, and new employees. Invest time to train people to do it your way - the right way - and then delegate it and let it go.

Developing satisfying personal relationships is something we all desire. To have a life full of love and a growing group of interesting friends is something we all want. My single friends are looking for the perfect partner to share the success and joys of life. Unfortunately, too many expect these relationships to develop by chance. To find new relationships I recommend becoming a more interesting person. Create yourself into something desirable. To do this, I suggest you learn a few new tricks. Become an expert in an area of interest like painting, computers, golf course design, or writing. Develop a business on the side or write a novel. Become more physically attractive by getting in shape and looking your best at every opportunity.

Becoming a person of action will make you more desirable to both sexes. I have always organized an annual golf tournament for friends and business associates to set myself apart from the average Joe. I once tried my hand at stand up comedy in an open mike night. I thrive on new educational experiences and have recently gotten the travel bug primarily because it makes me more interesting to others. Prepare an exciting answer to the question, "how are you doing?" and new relationships will find you.

Tip #3. Be the first to incorporate the latest and greatest. Take advantage of the latest technology to elevate your comfort zone. Computers can remove the tedious details from your life. Let your computer track when you have to make a phone call, send a proposal, or check up on an order. Introduce any technology, not just computer-related technology. Trade shows, industry specific literature, and competitors are great places to find new technology. It's everywhere.

Tip #4. Understand your body clock. Some of us are morning people and some of us are night owls. Identify when you are most alert during the day and conduct your most challenging activities during that time. Conduct administrative activities during your body's slow hours. Recognizing when you will be most productive and using that to your benefit will enhance your comfort zone.

Another way to maximize your time concerns a different type of down time. Time in traffic can be used to return phone calls or strategize. Listening to the news instead of your favorite music will make you more interesting and helpful to your clients and co-workers. Self-improvement tapes will also improve your production and make traffic less noticeable.

Tip #5. Keeping a customer is easier than finding a new one. Part of your comfort zone improvement should be to maintain a certain percentage of customers while attracting new ones. Covet your clients and do whatever it takes to keep them happy. Do not take them for granted. Real improvement should account for a high percentage of repeat business. If you open 10 accounts in year one, you should open 15 accounts in year two. If 5 of the 10 clients from year one remain, you should have 20 clients at the end of year two, not 15. Keeping customers is a great way to expand your comfort zone.

Tip #6. Add additional products and services. Increasing your offerings or expanding your product lines to existing clients is a great way to sell more with less effort. Try offering a service or maintenance package to your clients. (See Hole Number 4, Equipment.)

Your comfort zone should encompass a specific time period. I suggest a one- and five-year plan. One advantage we all have for expanding our comfort zone is that we typically get better at our job. Expand your comfort zone to get better results with the same effort.

"One thing about golf is you don't know why you play bad and why you play good.
- George Archer, Professional Golfer

The comfort zone is one characteristic that separates a golfer on the PGA tour from the rest of us. It is the type of golf that you play when you are not on fire and when you are not completely lost. It is what you normally shoot. The PGA tour players recondition their comfort zone so that shooting a 68 or 69 is a walk in the park. It is the mental adjustment to shoot lower scores using yesterday's concentration. It is also the gradual mental acceptance and expectation of better results.

Change should feel awkward. Making swing changes and course management changes should produce a feeling that something is different. Tempo, strategy, and swing changes should temporarily take you out of your existing comfort zone. If you do not experience a foreign feeling for some period, the changes you think you are making are probably not taking place. At this point you can expect the same results. Welcome and expect the feeling that something is wrong or different until the changes become a part of your new comfort zone. Over time the investment will be worth it. The initial awkwardness should be expected and not surprise you. Change is challenging.

Reconstruct your round. From a course management perspective, one way to expand your comfort zone on the golf course is to reconstruct your golf round from 18 holes to six 3-hole rounds. For instance, if your goal is to break 90, on each of the three-hole segments, you can allow yourself two bogeys and one par. Mentally approach the round this way and it becomes less overwhelming. If you are trying to break 80, give yourself one bogey and two pars every three holes. My father and I make bets in three-hole segments for this purpose.

Identify weaknesses. Find the area of your game that needs help and start there. Recognizing and attempting to improve your weaknesses will add confidence to your comfort zone. If you are having trouble getting up and down, practice your chipping until you can hit the shot with confidence. A small amount of practice will be noticed immediately. If you are struggling with your putter, be focused on simply two-putting. Develop ways to improve your concentration and be deliberate with your actions. Massage your comfort zone and elevate your mental cruise control so you are **comfortable** playing a better game.

"There is no such thing as natural touch. Touch is something you create by hitting millions of golf balls."
                    -Lee Trevino, professional golfer

The European Club's 17th at sunset can make you forget your name. Dublin, Ireland.

NUMBER 9 - FOLLOW THROUGH

"Follow-through" is like an alley-oop pass to yourself. If you're not a basketball fan, an alley-oop is a play where one player passes the ball just above the rim, the "alley." Another player catches the ball in mid-air and dunks it, the "oop." It's a spectacular play that relies on timing and the unexpected. Just like "follow-through." "Follow-through" is the "oop" in your execution. If you aren't willing to finish with style, why bother with the pass? "Follow-through" is your finishing, unexpected touch.

"Following through" is like shaving and showering, do it every day or you'll look like a bum.
This hole plays longer than its yardage and is the one hole on this course where you can make a big number if you're not careful. Let's get to the turn on a good note. On this hole you will learn that too many of us make soft commitments and avoid accountability. I will show you how firm commitments will impress strangers and get you into that meeting or sales call that has eluded you. I'll show you how to use "follow-through" to position a lost sale or promotion so you do not make the same mistake twice. You will also learn the value of finding everyone's passions to build new relationships and how to develop a picture-perfect follow-through with your golf swing.

"Follow-through" separates the rookies from the all-stars. Not following through in the office is similar to not following through on your golf swing. You lose impact. Your ideas don't get noticed. Prospects forget your name. The interviewer cannot distinguish you from the ten other candidates. "Follow through" helps you eliminate the possibility of wasting your time. And who can afford to waste time? OK, here we go.

"Follow-through" requires three things, **creativity**, **horse sense**, and **hustle**.

Creativity. We are all trying to separate ourselves from the pack and get noticed. Not only do we want to be noticed, we want to be remembered and desired. The easiest way to do this is to be a little different in your methods. Put a twist on your business, and give people something they are not expecting. There is a company called "Forms and Worms" that produces all kinds of preprinted paper forms. Their gimmick is dropping two or three plastic worms in every box of forms they ship. Hence, the name. How can you forget "Forms and Worms?" Hilarious.

Creativity helped me land an awesome part-time job with an advertising agency. Most people think the world is on vacation the whole month of December. I thought I might get lucky by being the only *one looking for a job around the holidays. I mailed custom Christmas cards describing my credentials in pure Yuletide fashion to the agencies that had the largest yellow page ads in the Atlanta phone book. I did not know a single person in the advertising business but thought it would be fun. I got two interviews and one job. Give the people what they are **not** expecting.*

THE WALL STREET JOURNAL.

Page B4.

MONEY & INVESTING

"Common sense is genius dressed in its working clothes."
- Ralph Waldo Emerson, American Author and Philosopher

s & Deal
Morgan, Chase

THU

Horse sense. Horse sense is the ability to look at every situation as if you were from a different planet, and ask the questions a child would ask. How often do you describe a situation and while you are describing what you have done, you realize you have made an air-headed, ridiculous blunder. We think ten steps ahead but forget step two. Talented business minds observe the obvious quite well. That's not meant to be sarcastic. Lack of horse sense is why a talented programmer can spend 10 days programming a feature that the customer does not want. Ever found yourself at the airport or the ballpark without your tickets? Have you ever nailed an interview for a great job and forgot to send a follow-up letter to show your colors? Horse sense can solve a lot of problems.

Hustle. Most "follow-through" activities are done after normal business hours. Thank you notes are a great example. There is not a one-to-one relationship between favors we do and thank you notes or calls that we get. That ratio is embarrassingly low. One "Thank You" activity each week will set you apart as a professional with "follow-through." If you want to "follow-through" make sure you follow-up. Send letters and e-mails confirming appointment times and places. Visit a client or supplier if you are in the neighborhood. Stopping for a cup of coffee with no agenda other than to say hello is always well received (even if they don't have time for you). Bring doughnuts to your morning meetings. Above all, do what you say you are going to do.

Most people do not do what they say they are going to do. If you say you are going to call somebody next week, make the call next week. Deadlines or specific timeframes for every activity demands "follow-through." Never end correspondence with an inexact, "I'll be in touch soon." Get **creative** and lock it up tight with an "I'll be in touch the morning of October 9." The challenge (**hustle**) now is for you to make that call on the morning of October 9. You have to make the call anyway (**horse sense**), so set yourself apart from the crowd in the cheap seats. It's the look-away pass before they sweep up the glass.

"Follow-through" gets attention, establishes credibility, and demonstrates your attention to detail. If you can tell a person you are going to do something at a specific time and actually do it, you've gotten their attention. Very few people actually do this. Why? I do not know. Second, you have gained instant credibility as a person who does what they say they are going to do! Third, they know you are exceptionally organized to actually pull off the trick. Fourth, they now know you are efficient with your time and very busy. And fifth, don't kid yourself, you will be the only one doing it. All this and they do not even know what you look like. If they have a pulse, of course they are free for lunch next week.

"People may doubt what you say, but they will believe what you do."
- Anonymous

When I was in college I met a "Beer Rep" visiting from the University of North Carolina. I went to school at Georgia Tech, and it being the geek capital of the ACC, there was no such thing. What exactly is a "Beer Rep" I asked? He explained that he represented Budweiser and made sure that all of the fraternities, sororities, and dorms had the necessary Budweiser party tools. He provided taps for kegs, neon lights, posters, assistance with beer trucks for the courtyard parties, and general marketing of Budweiser products.

*Cancel my classes I've got a new career! I drifted off into Wayne's World and saw myself at a party, handing out beer bongs with my picture on them. Women standing in line to get a beer from my beer truck, with my picture on it (**creativity**), and people asking for my autograph, and...and then the guy shook me and said I was drooling like a geek. I apologized for my trance and wished him good luck with Budweiser.*

*Possessed, I went to the local liquor store where everyone on campus bought beer. I asked the manager which brand of beer was the most popular (**horse sense**). He said his biggest "mover" was Pabst Blue Ribbon because it was the cheapest. I then asked him for the name and address of the distributor. General Wholesale Distributors, I remember it like it was yesterday.*

*First thing Monday morning I put on a suit, walked into General Wholesale Distributors, and asked for the owner, the top dog (**hustle**). This was waaaayy too important for a manager. I explained to the secretary that I was from Georgia Tech and I needed about five minutes of the owner's time and that, no, I did not have an appointment. Twenty seconds later I'm standing in front of the biggest desk I had ever seen. The president offered me a chair and I sat down. I said I had an inside connection to the social scene at Georgia Tech and I could help him "move" more product than he was currently "moving." At that moment the term "moving product" became etched into my brain as the greatest business expression of all time. His next question was perfect. "How much are you* *looking to get paid?" But not as perfect as my answer, "You don't have to pay me anything!" And we both laughed out loud. He turned out to be a great guy and said he'd pay me $25 a week and I could do whatever I wanted, so long as it "moved product"! I learned the beer business, some valuable sales lessons, and made sure I had plenty of samples on hand at all times.*

Like just about everything, "follow-through" requires action. When meeting someone for the first time, how about a little research (**horse sense**)? For initial sales calls or meetings, thoroughly investigate the company. Know their stock performance over the last 24 months. If it rocked or got rocked, research why. Stock performance impacts every employee in one way or another. Dig up (**hustle**) where they went to school, where they live, where they came from, or if they tee it up. Put on your detective hat and get **creative**. The objective is to find information other than what you are meeting about. I would rather talk about golf than anything. Everyone has something that they drop everything for. A few minutes of research and you will probably come up with it. People keep their passions close.

Now that you have the information, how you use it is also important. Timing is critical. Keep the information you have gathered to yourself for at least five or ten minutes into the meeting or it may lose its sincerity. Get down to business after the introductions. If everything is going smoothly, wait until the opportunity presents itself and slide the information in. If things are awkward or there is a period of silence, say, "This meeting was very important to (me /my company/ my family) and while I was preparing I learned that..."_____... and say whatever you learned. Let them know you cared enough to do a little personal research about them. You will be respected and remembered, and again, the only one doing it.

Learn why you lost. You can't close every deal. So what is your action plan for the losses? Here's what you do. Contact the prospect and insist on a debriefing (**hustle**). During that meeting, praise the competition for winning the business. Do not disparage them. They won and at this stage you are better off supporting the client's decision. Then, find out the details of what you did wrong. This meeting will help you in three ways. One, it will be the first step to rebuilding your relationship so that you are the first call they make when your competition botches the account. Two, you will be given the harsh reality of where you went wrong (**horse sense**). Your proposal may have been late or sloppy, your pricing may have been too high, your products may have missed their requirements, or you may have misunderstood their situation. Whatever you discover, you won't do it again. Third, you'll wipe the slate clean. Your professionalism will be what they remember when they need your products or services the next time around. Position yourself by losing gracefully and preparing to win next year.

"Follow-through" is a great way to display your creative muscle. Have some fun with it and develop your own ideas. To get started, do one thank-you activity per week, place time frames around every activity, and do a little extra research for important meetings. Be specific about all of your intentions, and demand it from those you do business with. "Follow-through" lets you make all the rules and puts space between you and the masses.

What your golf swing does after impact is as important as what it does before impact. Most golfers have a short "follow-through" after making contact with the ball. Our swings also have a tendency to get shorter as the day progresses and significantly shorter if we are playing poorly. A solid swing through the ball letting the club gradually slow down as it winds around your body will increase distance and accuracy. Try not to use any muscles to stop the club or "shortarm" the swing.

Most golfers fade or slice the ball. A good, full "follow-through" will reduce the cut on your shot significantly. Following through on your swing gives you the feeling of hitting through the ball as opposed to just hitting the ball.

Tension will shorten your "follow-through." Try to complete your swing with your back to your divot to ensure a full turn after contact. If you can force yourself to focus on your "follow-through" the club's tendency is to be more square at impact and the odds of it accelerating (not decelerating) through the ball are increased.

Your "follow-through" also tests your balance. A solid follow-through lets you finish with a pose. Lower handicap players, more often than not, have a long "follow-through" and finish balanced.

Following through helps your balance, but don't pose too long. The last tournament I played in, three-quarters of the field finished 55 minutes later than our group. I don't enjoy a five-hour round or eating alone. Slow play is taking the sport out of the game. Your pace of play is part of your "follow-through" responsibility. Figure out a way to complete your round in four hours or less (**creativity**). It is easy to get behind and inadvertently slow up the entire golf course (**horse sense**). Treat the game like any other sport (**hustle**). Do not take the sport out of the game for those behind you. Be deliberate with your actions. Find it, hit it, and find it again, but be back in the clubhouse in four.

Try to keep the "follow-through" thought throughout the round. Following through on putts will help you get the ball to the hole and keep you from decelerating the putt off-line. Following through on chips will help you avoid the chili-dip. A short "follow-through" seems to be a natural tendency in life. Focus on your "follow-through" and you will hit it longer and straighter both on and off the golf course.

"Success seems to be largely a matter of hanging on after others have let go."

—William Feather, U.S. Author and Publisher

Getting ready for the turn. Gary Player Country Club and Spa's 9th green. Sun City, South Africa.

The Turn

Nice nine, keep it up and you may set the course record. Before you get to the tenth tee, make a plan for how you are going to use what you discovered on the front side. Take a seat in the grill and enjoy some food for thought. Put it on my tab.

Take your time, you have got the course to yourself.

"There are two things to aim at in life: first, to get what you want; and after that, to enjoy it. Only the wisest of mankind achieve the second."
    - *Logan Pearsall Smith, writer and critic*

"Keep your sense of humor. There's enough stress in the rest of your life to let bad shots ruin a game you're supposed to enjoy."
    - *Amy Alcott, Professional Golfer*

"Nothing goes down slower than a golf handicap."
    - *Bobby Nichols, Professional Golfer*

"When one thing is working, it helps the next thing. You just go from strength to strength."
    - *Greg Norman, Professional Golfer*

"Don't be ashamed of choking...any golfer who has never choked on the golf course should be in an asylum. . . Sooner or later all normal human beings encounter situations on the course that they are not, at that particular moment, emotionally capable of handling."
    - *Paul Runyan, Professional Golfer*

"When you miss a shot, never think of what you did wrong. Come up to the next shot thinking of what you must do right."
    - *Tommy Armour, Professional Golfer*

"In thirty years we're going to be in our 90's. We're going to play three-hole tournaments for $900,000 and the one who remembers his score wins."
    - *Bob Bruce, Professional Golfer on the senior tour*

"The dollars aren't so important - once you have them."
    - *Johnny Miller, Professional Golfer*

"Approach the golf course as a friend, not an enemy."
    - *Arnold Palmer, Professional Golfer*

"I played the tour in 1967 and told jokes and nobody laughed. Then I won the Open the next year, told the same jokes, and everybody laughed like hell."
  - Lee Trevino, Professional Golfer

"Thinking instead of acting is the number one golf disease."
  - Sam Snead, Professional Golfer

"The game just embarrasses you until you feel inadequate and pathetic. You want to cry like a child."
  - Craig Stadler, Professional Golfer

"You'll never increase your driving distance without a positive mental attitude. Confidence is vital."
  - Greg Norman, Professional Golfer

"Pay no attention to what the critics say; there has never been a statue erected to a critic."
  - Jean Sibelius, Composer

"Of all the hazards, fear is the worst."
  - Sam Snead, Professional Golfer

"Men make counterfeit money; in many more cases, money makes counterfeit men."
  - Sidney J. Harris, Author

"The toughest thing for most people to learn in golf is to accept the bad holes - and then forget about them."
  - Gary Player, Professional Golfer

"A great round of golf is a lot like a terrible round. You drift into a zone, and it is hard to break out of it."
  - Al Geiberger, Professional Golfer

"Any fact facing us is not as important as our attitude toward it, for that determines our success or failure."
  - Norman Vincent Peale, Philosopher and Author

"Pain and suffering are inevitable in our lives, but misery is an option."
   - Chip Beck, Professional Golfer

"Undirected practice is worse than no practice. Too often you become careless and sloppy in your swing. You'd be better off staying home and beating the rugs."
   - Gary Player, Professional Golfer

"We all choke. You just try to choke last."
   - Tom Watson, Professional Golfer

"There is no limit to what can be accomplished when no one cares who gets the credit."
   - John Wooden, NCAA basketball coach

"Action before thought is the ruination of most of your shots."
   - Tommy Armour, Professional Golfer

"The best thing about giving of ourselves is that what we get is always better than what we give. The reaction is greater than the action."
   - Orison Swett Marden, Author

"Long irons take longer to happen, so ease off and allow the swing to happen."
   - Corey Pavin, Professional Golfer

"Wherever you see a successful business, someone once made a courageous decision."
   - Peter Drucker, father of modern management philosophy

"One thing you don't ever do is think of bad things when you're over a ball. People might think about bad shots, but I don't - even on shots I might be scared to hit."
   - Fred Couples, Professional Golfer

"Excellence is the gradual result of always striving to do better."
   - Pat Riley, NBA Coach

"Some men go through a forest and see no firewood."
    - English proverb

"There is far more opportunity than there is ability."
    - Thomas Edison, Inventor of the lightbulb and phonograph

"I am a slow walker, but I never walk backwards."
    - Abraham Lincoln, United States President

"Many of life's failures are people who did not realize how close they were to success when they gave up."
    - Thomas Edison, Inventor of the lightbulb and phonograph

"You may have to fight a battle more than once to win it."
    - Margaret Thatcher, first female Prime Minister of Great Britain

"A part of control is learning to correct your weaknesses."
    - Babe Ruth, Professional Baseball Player

"Nothing good comes in life or athletics unless a lot of hard work has preceded the effort. Only temporary success is achieved by taking short cuts."
    - Roger Staubach, NFL quarterback, sports broadcaster

"I'd like to be known as a gentleman first, and then as a golfer. That's all."
    - Ben Hogan, Professional Golfer on how he'd like to be remembered

"A long drive is good for the ego."
    - Arnold Palmer, Professional Golfer

"Sports do not build character. They reveal it."
    - Heywood Hale Broun, writer

"One of the advantages bowling has over golf is that you seldom lose a bowling ball."
  - Don Carter, champion bowler

"When you have confidence, you can have a lot of fun; and when you have fun, you can do amazing things."
  - Joe Namath, Professional Football player

"I don't say my golf game is bad, but if I grew tomatoes, they'd come up sliced."
  - Miller Barber, Professional Golfer

"When all is said and done, as a rule, more is said than done."
  - Lou Holtz, NCAA Football coach

"People who enjoy what they are doing invariably do it well."
  - Joe Gibbs, NFL head coach

"Class is an intangible quality which commands, rather than demands, the respect of others."
  - John Wooden, NCAA Basketball coach

"Golf is the hardest game in the world. There is no way you can ever get it. Just when you think you do, the game jumps up and puts you in your place."
  - Ben Crenshaw, Professional Golfer

"A bad attitude is worse than a bad swing."
  - Payne Stewart, Professional Golfer

Ignore the distractions on the par 3, 3rd at Emerald Dunes. West Palm Beach, Florida.

NUMBER 10 – THE LEADER BOARD

"How would you like to meet the top 143 people at what you do each week in order to survive?"

- Bruce Crampton, Professional Golfer

More information is always better than less information. Always.

Similar to the tour, there are plenty of Leader Boards in your life. Not big white ones with names and scores on them, but unlimited information right in front of you. This is, after all, the information age. Information is everywhere, but you have to look at it, learn from it, and use it to make better decisions. This hole will help you find the Leader Boards in your life and show you how to use them. It is like cheating on a test with the teacher's permission.

This hole is a short par three. The easiest hole on the course. Here you will be reminded that you can gain a significant edge by finding and using new information wisely. You will see that emulating the habits of other successful people is a shortcut to your own success. I will also show you how to use your competitors as a tool for your professional growth. You will see your surroundings on the golf course much differently after playing this hole, and you will never play another round without your own personal Leader Board.

Pay attention to what's going on around you. Information is the new currency of power and success. Like dollar bills on the sidewalk, pick up as much information as you can.

Learn from competitors. Of all the Leader Boards in your career, the most important one concerns your competition. The person with the most information **always** wins. Know what your competition is doing, who they are hiring, and when they are introducing a bigger, better deal. The famous BBD. Know their strengths and weaknesses, and know exactly how to beat them. If you can't beat them, you may want to join them.

Every business is competing for every dollar against something. Know what you are competing with or who you are competing against. If it is a direct competitor, know their product line. Moreover, if they are doing something good, as long as you can copy it, copy it. Just because it was not your idea does not mean it is not a good idea. Use all of your competitor's good ideas. They are using yours.

Be on competitor's mailing lists and view their websites a few times each week. Knowing your competition better than anyone in your company provides great job security, and you will reduce your chances of getting caught sleeping at the wheel. Then use the information as you need it. After you have your competition in your corner, learn about your clients and prospective clients. Be on their mailing lists and visit their websites. You can be "In the Know" or "In the No." The difference is information.

A reputation as someone with inside information is a good reputation to have for a variety of reasons. You may even be considered an expert when you drop the ship date of your competitors new offering or know the name of the latest employee who jumped ship or came aboard. Clients are also a great source of information about your competitors. Asking a lot of questions and listening is a fact-gathering technique that will yield quite a bit of information about the competition's weaknesses.

The Internet has placed almost all of the world's information at your fingertips. Train yourself to use the tool of the 21st century. Until you do, never admit to being computer illiterate, even if you are. And certainly do not blurt it out when there is not a computer in sight, it only has negative consequences. Some old-schoolers wear the self-proclaimed computer illiterate label like a badge of courage. That badge certainly will not get you a promotion or more business. Eventually you've got to get off the horse and learn to drive. Get your kids to teach you, but find a way to get the information of the Internet in your hands.

*I was working for IBM when their first Personal Computer was introduced. I watched the evolution from the dual floppy drive to the first hard drive, from DOS to Windows, and stand-alone systems to the first PC networks. I witnessed the rise of the popularity of the Personal Computer from 1984 to 1990. It was **easy** to recognize that the wave was just beginning. One observation was that the weak* *link in the success of the PC was the task of developing software. At the time, software tools were at the fire and stick stage. Now you can design your own web site in an hour practically for free. That was not the case in 1990. Web sites and the Internet were still cult concepts as late as 1994. The world jumped in around 1995. If there was ever an opportunity to get in early, the software game was it. At the time, PC software applications for businesses were quite clumsy compared to the options, ease of use, and speed of today's programs. Every business needed software, and there was always someone willing to pay for quality software applications. In 1990 I left IBM and started a software development firm because the Leader Board told me to. All the information was right in front of me. I am proud to say the corporation I founded is in its 11th year of growth under new management and has thrived quite well without my input. Knowing when to sell the business was also on the Leader Board.*

Know where you stand. Know where you rank in relation to your colleagues and professional peers. Do not be at (or close to) the bottom of the totem pole. If you are not next in line for the promotion, find out who is. Be proactive and ask your boss where you stand. Like they say, "If you don't know who the sucker is at the poker table, you're the sucker." Do not be the weak link in your office.

Not only do you want to pay attention to where you stand, but also pay attention to where you stand based on your growth goals defined earlier in this book. In business it is Grow or Die. If all you are doing is matching last year's numbers, you are on a path to going under. Make sure your Leader Board encompasses your growth.

"Would you rather be broke or have money in the bank?"
- Ben Hogan, professional golfer, when asked if he would rather be in the lead or a shot or two behind going into the last round

Follow the money. It solves crimes and answers the question, Why?, in almost every situation. Money talks, so listen and act accordingly. It is why the market is always correct and bookies hit the spread dead-on every time. Money is the great equalizer and can get you to the "brass tacks" of any situation faster than any other method.

Watch and understand the finances surrounding your job. Are you a good investment for your company? Are the shareholders getting a great return on your salary? Where are you against quota? How is the company positioned? Have your customers paid, or are they past due? Can you meet payroll and your other financial commitments? How are your clients' finances? How is Wall Street treating your firm? The most valuable employees keep an eye on the financial Leader Board.

Emulate success. You also want to know who is on the Leader Board. Identify people you feel are successful. It may include financial success, a well-balanced family life, or a challenging career. Whatever your definition of success, find those that have achieved similar success and emulate them. Success is okay to copy. Do not be too proud to make changes in your life that emulates others.

If I were a professional basketball player, I would find out what time Michael Jordan got to the gym. I would find out what he ate before games and before workouts. I would find out his exercise program. I would put on his Air Jordan's and just do it. If you want to be the best, there is nothing like acting like the best. Envision yourself at the top of that leader board.

The people above you on the Leader Board are the ones that work a little harder. They always look like they are in the right place at the right time, and that everything is given to them. Well, I have got news for you, that is not the case. They are as lost and nervous as you are underneath. They are also not that much different from you, but they are out-hustling you. They get close to decision-makers. They produce. They are comfortable with their abilities and they are comfortable talking to the CEO.

"In business, the competition will bite you if you keep running; if you stand still, they will swallow you."

- Semon Knudsen, General Motors vice-president

THE WALL ST

n profit **Page B4**

I thought you might enjoy this unique perspective of the Leader Board. If we could shrink the world's population to a village of 100 people, it would look like this:

There would be 57 Asians, 21 Europeans, 14 from the Western Hemisphere, and 8 Africans.

51 would be female.

70 would be non-white.

70 would be non-Christian.

50 percent of the world's wealth would be in the hands of only 6 people, and all 6 would be citizens of the United States.

80 people would live in substandard housing.

30 would be unable to read.

50 would suffer from malnutrition.

1 would be near death, 1 near birth.

1 would have a college education.

No one would own a computer.

- Bill Campbell, January 13, 1998
    Fort Walton Beach Daily News

You and I don't play golf with an eye on the Leader Board because we are not on tour and six-inch, red letters of our scores posted is similar to that dream about going to work naked. Our Leader Board refers to all of the information that surrounds you on the golf course.

How many times have we seen PGA players not watch the leader board and do something silly? Jean Van de Velde needed a double bogey six to win the British Open in 1999. He took a seven and lost it in a playoff. Jesper Parnevic in the 1994 British Open at Turnberry comes to mind. He went for a difficult pin on the 18th hole when all he needed was a par to win. He ended up making a bogey and losing by one stroke to Nick Price. One stroke.

I understand the reason for not counting strokes against par early in a round or tournament, but down the stretch, information can only help you.

Information removes doubt. People who do not want all the information that they could possibly have before making a decision will always be the underdog. The more information you have, the more comfortable you are going to feel about a decision. For instance, get an exact distance for a break on a putt before you actually stroke the putt. How many times do you stroke a putt without an exact break in mind and hope it goes in? Have an exact target line before you pull the putter back. I have not wished a putt into the hole yet.

"You have three doubles and a triple before the seventh inning (+10). You have three doubles and a triple before the 5th hole (-20). You have three doubles and a triple before work (-50)."
- Rick Reilly, sportswriter, on keeping score in life,
Sports Illustrated, October 1998

Absorbing all of the nuances on the golf course will eliminate mental mistakes including misclubbing, incorrect yardage, elevation and wind changes, and avoiding hazards and trouble spots. When hitting shots, know where you **do not** want to be. Factor in the wind, lie, and hazards before you pull the trigger. It is simple, but how often do we miss the obvious?

Be aware of the dynamics around you. Do not let other players in your foursome affect your game. It's inevitable that you'll be paired with somebody who will click their teeth or rattle their clubs or have some type of annoying habit that's going to get under your skin. Be aware that it is happening and ignore it.

Adjust your pace. Slow play and the occasional rainstorm are part of the game. The best thing about slow play is that at least you are still playing. Do not let slow play get in your head, just factor it into your tempo. Take more time over the ball, expand your pre-shot routine, and think a little longer about what you are doing. Do not fall for the slow play excuse. Let your competition lose their game. More than the score is posted on the leader board.

"Study the green as you approach it."
- Tom Watson, Professional Golfer

Information shapes goals. Know what your goal is for each swing and each hole. If you are playing in a tournament or match and a bogey wins it, make that bogey. Do not try to make birdie, take a double and not win. Pay attention to the leader board. It is easy to do and you will have a better chance of accomplishing your objectives.

Do not let your ego blind you from the Leader Board. More information is always better than less information. Always.

The kangaroos are friendly companions on Joondalup Country Club's Quarry Course. Perth, Western Australia.

NUMBER 11 - KNOW YOUR PARTNER

"Coming together is a beginning, staying together is progress, and working together is success."
Henry Ford, Ford Motor Company founder, inventor of the assembly line manufacturing concept, and first to share profits with employees

Loan me a tee and I'll grab your driver, we're going to play this hole as a team. A little backup is great for relieving pressure! That is just one reason why partnerships are great. Together, you and I will see a few reasons why a partnership is not about giving up half but about gaining half. We will discuss what you should know about your partner and outline the characteristics of successful partnerships. I will teach you the benefits of a team approach and how to handle those inevitable forks in the road. There are also potential partners waiting to be discovered in all areas of your business life. I have done this before, so just hang in the shade if you want; I've got you covered on this one.

The most common partnership in America is marriage. Marriage can be a significant emotional and financial partnership, but it is also so much more. This chapter outlines business partnership guidelines, some of which can be applied to your marriage and personal relationships. The National Center for Health Statistics gathers marriage and divorce data, and the numbers are about what you have heard. In 1998 there were 2,072,000 marriages and 870,000 divorces; in 1997 there were 2,219,000 marriages and 1,059,000 divorces. These two years combined represent 45 divorces for every 100 marriages. Because the number of marriages is increasing, some authorities estimate the divorce rate to be as high as 57%. The average length of new marriages is 26 months. These are ridiculously low success rates! Your probability for partnership success will increase significantly if you take the following simple suggestions seriously.

Most of us have considered starting a business with a friend, business colleague, or being in a partnership with a group. Without partnerships, many offerings in the market would not exist. At the root of every merger and acquisition is the belief that combining company services, markets, or products will result in a more competitive organization. Large corporations have certainly seen the value of partnerships. Now because you are not a corporation, and I recognize that different configurations for partnerships can exist, we'll keep it simple and evaluate partnership roles with you being one of the principals in a 50-50 partnership.

Complementary skills. A typical partnership consists of: "I will make 'em if you can sell 'em." The most basic ingredient for a successful partnership is the combining of complementary skills. Partners who do not have complementary skills will soon be competitors. Make sure that your partners offer something that you **cannot** or **do not** want to offer without them. If you can get by without them, then get by without them. If you cannot, a partnership is the only answer.

Trust. The second requirement for a successful partnership is trust. Do not collaborate with someone you do not trust. The best partnership agreements are based on a handshake and a verbal agreement. Do not be afraid to trust people. Most people are trustworthy. Trust people until they take advantage of you. Most will not. When they do, cut them off quickly, quietly, and permanently. Word will get around that you play by the rules, and people will want to be your partner.

Commitment. Another critical component of a successful partnership is an equal work ethic or commitment to the partnership. One of the quickest ways to break up a partnership is to have one partner on the golf course and one partner in the office. It does not take long for that to break down. Be comfortable with each partner's level of commitment.

Partnerships can get complicated when it comes to who is doing what. Having open communication is critical. Discuss very clearly what is expected from each partner and be comfortable with the arrangement. Always pull your end of the bargain or you will be replaced before you know what hit you. Be flexible to change as your partnership environment changes, but do not alter your agreed upon expectations without concurrence. One partner changing the rules confuses everyone.

Similar lifestyles. You will also have a better chance for success if you and your partner have similar distractions outside of the partnership. Two people with families will work better than one single person and one married person. My partner and I were single and could be at the office all night if the situation arose (Dark-thirty, as we called it, and it happened more than I ever imagined it would). Account for your personal lives before entering a partnership. Similar lifestyles enhance a partnership.

Do not think small. In any partnership, things will never be even-steven. Over the long haul, the nickels and dimes work out. If you are keeping score along the way, you may drive yourself crazy. A couple hundred dollars between partners is chump change in the bigger picture. If you are a bigger picture kind of person, a partnership should work for you. If you split your dinner checks based on who ordered what, a business partnership might not be your best bet.

Share. The fear of sharing can kill a partnership or keep one from getting off the ground. Don't forget that **half of a lot is still a lot**. There will be times where you add more value than your partner, but that is the essence of partnership, and it does not work without you both, so put the whining towel away.

"To get the full value of a joy you must have somebody to divide it with."
- Mark Twain, American author

You may be able to eventually accomplish your goals without a partner, but you may not have as much fun. A good partner is a great asset because you double the number of eyes watching the shop. Partners share the risk and the successes. Without a partner, you have to come up with all the good ideas (not to mention all of the money). That is pressure.

Two heads are always better than one. The problem with two heads is that sometimes they head-butt. Make sure that you and your partner can butt heads without killing each other. Be prepared to be criticized and be prepared to criticize. Accept these criticisms as suggestions for the good of the whole, which they are. Being wrong or making mistakes is never easy. When you do butt heads, be open-minded enough to listen to the other side of the story.

My business started when my best friend, who is still my best friend, and I decided to write and sell software. He would write the programs and I would sell them. It was a little more complicated than that, but not much. Our first argument happened over some perceptions, or misconceptions, concerning our arrangement. When incorporating, the state requires that all corporations have a president and vice president, secretary, and other documented corporate positions. We discussed that at this stage it did not matter who was who, so I signed as President, and he signed for the other positions. No big deal, right? Well, it wasn't, until someone told my partner that, "He had heard that I had declared myself president and how could he let me wrestle control from him? etc... etc." I never insinuated or said those things, but people will try to burst your bubble won't they? Had I heard those things I probably would have become suspicious as well. My partner held his tongue as long as he could, and then he exploded. I had no idea what had happened. Once he told me what had happened, I explained that I had not said any of those things, did not think them, that none of it mattered, and that we should change the documents immediately. We agreed to rotate the positions every year and did it the first year, but after that it became a tiresome exercise. Like most misunderstandings, it was forgotten about quickly. The challenge of meeting payroll put the issue into its proper perspective. We never had an altercation on that level again. Outside influences and emotions can introduce problems if your lines of communication are blocked.

Be prepared for opposition and ill will from outside influences. Jealousy and doubt can rain on your partnership. Ask questions before you let someone or something get between you and your partner. Manage your relationship with your partner as a very real component of your business.

Keep your legal documents to a minimum until you start making money. You and your partner can itemize your partnership any way you want. Just write it down in plain English. The legal profession has blackmailed us into thinking that we have to sign a legal document every time we go to the bathroom. You do not.

A partnership can destroy friends and families, but if you do not let friction turn to fire you will be fine. Deal face-to-face with partners on any issue, and ask, "How should we handle it?" Be generous and be fair. As long as you agree that you will negotiate fairly, honestly, and with the goals of the business or the partnership in mind, you will make it work.

Partnerships can be created if you are looking in the right places. You deal with people on a weekly basis that may be able to help you advance your business, but we forget to ask. Your dry cleaner, car dealer, landlord or real estate broker, or any other person that you conduct business with can be potential clients or, at the very least, a great reference. If you

The wind is a permanent partner on the the 7th hole of Balybunion's New Course. Balybunion, Ireland.

buy your home or cars from one person or company, the owner should know you. If your business applies to him or her, ask them to support your business as you have supported theirs. At the very least, ask them if you can use them as a reference. Instant partner. Ask your dry cleaner if you can put your business flyers on the bulletin board. By giving our business to people, we may be able to capitalize on a relationship that can grow significantly. We all enjoy bending over backward for our clients. Another suggestion is to offer yourself as a reference for anyone that impresses you. Again, instant partner, and the start of a relationship with your definition of a winner.

In marriage and business, have a clear understanding of both parties' expectations. Trust your partners and believe that you can work together on a daily basis, and that both partners are willing to sacrifice equally to achieve your goals. Use these checks to increase your odds for partnership success.

Playing as a team on the golf course is a riot. However, make sure you have the right partner.

I am not completely sold on this handicap system. I have seen too many 15s shoot 75. (I wonder if they give shrug lessons?) A golf handicap is the easiest way to cheat that I have ever seen in any sport. Golf is the only game where they let someone who could not beat you without strokes, wax you. I am all for helping my fellow man, but geez. How about a handicap system for hoops? When the boys are dunking on me I could use a little help. Right? "Next."

Golf is so hard we have got to help the lousy players. And we're all lousy. Remember that a high handicapper can absolutely beat your brains in. If you are playing with a high handicapper that you have never played with before, watch out! I am not saying people with high handicaps are less honest than the lower handicaps. Just make sure you know what your partner is capable of before you get involved in a match or a bet.

Play your own game. To be successful in partner competition, play your game and forget about your partner. If you play well, your team will play well. If you start relying on your partner when you're in your pocket, you are going to put too much stress on the team. Play as if you are playing your own ball.

"Don't praise your own good shots. Leave that function to your partner who, if a good sport, will not be slow in performing it."
- Harry Vardon, English golfer and father of the modern golf swing

Have fun. Make sure you have fun with your partner on the course, the whole time. It is all about fun. Use the opportunity to solidify your friendship. Laugh off the bad breaks and never get mad at your partner during a match. Do not let your partner cheat. Keep an eye on your partner because your integrity is also at stake. If you find yourself in a situation where your partner is bending the rules, simply clarify that you want to win but not that badly. They will get the message.

Before making a team wager, make sure you and your partner are clear on what the rules of the bet are, and how much you are playing for. Bet only what the two of you are willing to lose. Do not put your partner in a situation where they may be forced to risk more money than they are comfortable losing. Nothing can put friction between you and your partner like putting them in a situation that he or she is not ready for.

Play in as many partner tournaments as you can. The competition in team format is great. Nevertheless, keep an eye on those high handicappers - "Next!"

12th Tee ➡

I've chipped in a few times on the 12th green at King's Creek Country Club. Rehoboth Beach, Delaware.

NUMBER 12 - CHIP IN

THE "WALL STREET JOURNAL"   THUR

"Continuous effort—not strength or intelligence—is the key to unlocking our potential."
Winston Churchill, British Leader, World War I and II

Deals **& Deal M**
Morgan, Chase

it **Page B4.**

MONEY & INVESTING

Chipping in is always a pleasant surprise. Not only on the golf course but also in your life and career. If you play this hole properly, your fifteen minutes of fame could last a lifetime. This hole is a long par five that requires you to plan for your third shot before you hit your second. Making par

on this hole requires a bit of extra planning and effort. Your popularity is based strictly on the value that you add or your willingness to "chip in" to every situation. Here, you will learn that unless you bring something to every relationship, every meeting, and every social event, your presence has little or no value. You will also discover why some guests are invited back and others are not. I'll be happy to let you borrow these ideas but only if you return them safely. Keep it down the middle here and you will never show up anywhere empty-handed again. I'll also provide instructions on how to "chip in" on every round of golf that you will ever play.

Always add value. What you "chip in" are your contributions to anything and everything that you touch. Make tangible, describable contributions to your career, your social life, your relationships, and your passions, and monitor the value that you are adding to the world around you. The world is full of people who have their hand out. I am not referring to the poor or homeless, but to the professional men and women pretending to be helpless and looking for others to pull their weight. They loathe accountability and commitment. They creep around like a bad odor. Beggars can be found in every occupation and in every wardrobe. Fall into this category and you can kiss success good-bye.

My wife has a great way to remind her clients of the value she adds. Adding value can be expressed using a variety of techniques, but this one always works.

Maintain a listing of all of your clients' and friends' industries and interests. Keep an eye out for articles or information that you come across in newspapers, magazines, or on the web that may affect them. News about competitors, industry trends, changes in your industry that may affect their business, or any information that may apply to them professionally or personally. Then mail them a copy with a "thought you might be interested" post-it.

This technique is great to remind your clients and friends that you do add value. These articles have no immediate relevance or impact on your business but may help your client. Your competition certainly is not practicing this technique. Feel free to use e-mail to share this information, but avoid mass e-mails. Forwarding e-mails and information impersonally will backfire. A hard copy letter has a more personal touch. This "chip in" technique is maximized with a personal, one-to-one exchange of information. This sends the message, "I am looking out for you even when I have nothing to gain."

Remembering birthdays or special events has the same effect. Although it is more personal than professional, the gesture is just as welcome. Try to use this example to remind your clients, friends, bosses, and co-workers of the value that you add.

It is simple math; you either add or subtract. In business, everything is, appropriately, categorized as an asset or a liability. Assets add and liabilities subtract. Breaking even counts as a liability. One of my favorite business expressions is "bring something." What you bring determines whether you are an asset or a liability. What are you bringing? Treat your life like a covered dish supper. If you don't bring a dish, you don't deserve to eat.

THE WALL STREET JOURNAL

MARKETPLACE

"Dependent people need others to get what they want. Independent people can get what they want through their own efforts. Interdependent people combine their own efforts with the efforts of others to achieve their greatest success."
- Steven Covey, Author, 7 Habits of Highly Effective People

Evaluate your friends. Friends that rely too heavily on you to carry their social lives may be holding you back. Socialize with friends that share in adding value to the relationship. If your friends do not offer inspiration and options, you may be pulled back instead of pushed forward. Distance yourself from the liabilities in your social circle.

If you sponge off life, you become easy to resent. Freeloaders become the running office joke. They, at best, are tolerated but never desired. Important projects are diverted away from them and

A chip shot is an acceptable alternative to the variety of other trouble surrounding Erinvale Country Club's 9th green. Cape Town, South Africa.

their opinions are never sought. They are people who "need a drink" when you are buying a round but then quietly order one for only themselves on the way back from the bathroom. I know that someone specific is in your mind right now. These people are dead weight. On the bright side, dead weight is always the first thing eliminated. If you are just standing around, you become an obstacle. Any obstacle on our way to success is resented.

You will never know. Understand that no one is going to tell you that you do not add value. You have to figure this out on your own. If your phone calls are not returned, or your circle of friends seems to be shrinking, or you are consistently the runner-up for the promotion, or no one notices your absence, you may be guilty of adding no value. Like bad breath or bad manners, explaining the concept of worthless to someone is easier to avoid than confront.

Prepare something for every meeting. Even if you only bring donuts, at least bring **something**. Invest **some** time preparing for all of your meetings. Showing up counts for nothing, and a small amount of preparation will be noticed and will maximize everyone's time.

Earn your business. Nothing is more pitiful than watching business people beg for recognition, credit, or a client's support. Looking for a free ride is a great way to get run over. If you assisted in the deal, split the commission. If the deal squeaked in your territory but was the result of someone else's work, do the right thing and back off. Be responsible for your own success by expecting to earn it instead of having it gifted to you.

"Send me the bill" is not enough. If you accidentally break something that does not belong to you, it is quite arrogant to merely say "send me the bill." Of course, saying nothing is worse. "Send me the bill" is equivalent to saying, "I broke your/our _____, you track down the number, schedule the service call, arrange to have it picked up or shipped, pay the bill, and then leave me your address, and I'll try to send you a check that does not bounce." "Chip in" and burden yourself with all of the hassles resulting from your carelessness.

Borrow generously. How you borrow things is an indication of your willingness to "chip in." I loaned my car to a friend once and he returned it with mud caked inside and out, the tank on empty, and a cup of coffee soaked into the carpet. He dropped one more ball and never acknowledged the mess. Twenty-five dollars and forty-five minutes later, it only looked like half a cup but still smelled like two. Return borrowed items immediately and clean them, lubricate them, and top off all of their tanks. Do this and friends will let you borrow just about anything.

A lazy guest is a lousy guest. Entertaining friends can be depressing. You may see traits in your friends that you would rather not see. When invited anywhere, bring a thoughtful gift to celebrate the hospitality and position yourself for future invitations. Examples include your host's favorite beverage or a gift associated with their hobby. Spend 10 minutes preparing something for them before you arrive. If your host is not present, leave something for them. Leave things cleaner than you found them or talk to your host specifically about the cleaning arrangements. Bring what you think you will consume plus a little extra. Generosity never goes bad. Guests who show up empty handed and expect their host to provide everything, obviously, are not chipping in and aren't much fun to entertain.

If you only call people when you need something, you will be denied and laughed at after they hang up the phone. Do not ask for two favors in a row. Going to the well for someone twice makes me feel used. Do not call long-lost friends and ask for favors unless you are good friends. Routinely stay in touch with your friends who can help you. It is an investment that everyone appreciates and a solid "chip in" move.

"Chipping in" is your commitment to the team concept. A team player is welcome everywhere. Freeloaders ride the bench. Give your company and colleagues more than they are expecting. Consistently add value and promotions and popularity will follow.

Chipping in on the golf course is a freebie. You never expect it and it always gets a smile. Drop these suggestions in your bag to "chip in" on your next round.

Turn your cell phone off. I have never seen a cell phone improve anyone's round, however, I have seen cell phones destroy a few. Checking voicemail is rarely going to be good for your golf game. If you must stay in contact with your office, use your cell phone sparingly and walk well away from your group. The golf course is our escape from the pressures of the office. Combining the two may compromise your playing partners' enjoyment.

Be sensitive to time commitments. Get to the course early or call and tell your group to tee off without you. This can make for an awkward start to the round, so make sure you are not consistently running to the first tee.

If you are being held up waiting for the last member of the group, try to wait if your time commitments and the course will allow it. I have had friends selfishly tee off early and make me catch them on the third hole. Not because I was late, they were just ready to go. Moreover, they called me to play.

Make any time constraints that you have known to your group. If you can only play nine, or if you have an important dinner or meeting after the round, let everyone know ahead of time. I would rather pick up the pace than have a member of my foursome have to leave on the 15th hole.

Do not quibble over strokes. Trying to obtain an unfair advantage with your handicap is sinister and eliminates the element of sport. Pros can shoot 67 today and 77 tomorrow. The spread is greater for the rest of us. Negotiate with fun in mind and set the number of strokes that will motivate you to play your best. Net 59s make everyone point and whisper. "Chip in" to the enjoyment of the competition and handicap yourself with a conscience. Winning a hole with a shot is a hollow victory anyway.

Don't complain. We've heard it all before. The course and conditions are what they are and even Augusta has room for improvement. Golfers from time to time think that they are the perfect specimen in the imperfect world around them. The beverage cart cannot personally follow each foursome, and caddies may misread a putt from time to time. If you are so good, why can't you tell when the putt is misread and why didn't you hit it closer in the first place? Triple bogeys are your own fault, and grass never jumps up and blocks your ball from the hole. Do us all a favor and minimize the commentary for your bad breaks.

Tip the help. When was the last time you ate at a restaurant and left no tip? I will bet you can remember playing golf and not tipping the staff. The staff of a golf course is as concerned with the enjoyment of your round as the wait staff is with the satisfaction of your meal. They rely on tips as a large percentage of their income. Make sure you "tip in" to "chip in" for the bag staff, caddies, and cart attendants.

And, of course, chip one in.

13th Tee ➡

Balance your emotions as the lake taunts you on the 7th hole of Big Horn's Mountain Course. Palm Springs, California.

NUMBER 13 – BALANCE

"If you break 100, watch your golf. If you break 80, watch your business."
- Joey Adams, Comedian

Balance is the pedestal of strength. Balance in our lives, our emotions, our decisions, and our activities are critical to keep fresh ideas flowing. With all of the options in today's world, you will see on the following pages that most of our actions inherently limit our options. On this hole we will review your balance and test your flexibility. I will show you how financial imbalance can become a powerful, silent burden that is easily eliminated. Don't swing too hard, and you will see how the status quo can take away independent thinking, why your boss is always right, and that most of us are not as balanced as we think we are. I will also show you how balance is a form of strength in our careers and our golf game.

Know more than your job. Balance, as a source of strength, in your career requires you to learn more about your industry and infrastructure. To grow as a professional, learn about what you **do not do** to set yourself apart. The marketing director who understands production is more valuable than the one who only understands marketing. You may find that your company's production technique is the best way to market your products. If you are involved strictly in sales, make a few friends in the shipping department, and spend some time with accounts receivable to understand the collection issues in your business. Educate yourself on shareholder issues and stock performance. The more you know about everybody's job, the better prepared you are to do yours.

"People think that at the top there isn't much room. They tend to think of it as an Everest. My message is that there is tons of room at the top."
- Margaret Thatcher, British Prime Minister

Maintain balance by keeping your firm's big picture, or primary objective, in mind. Start with the company's mission statement. If you cannot find one, it is time to write one. Learn and think about the objectives of your boss, your boss's boss, the president, and the shareholders or owners. Put yourself in the owners' position and solve problems with their objectives in mind. With the goals of the organization in mind, you will always make the right decisions.

Your boss is right. Your company is not there to advance your career, you are there to advance your company's interests. As long as you accomplish the objectives of everyone above you in the chain of command, your company will have no choice but to return the favor. As you review the responsibilities up the management chain, a larger variety of variables have to be satisfied at each level. When we are given assignments that seem ludicrous, take into consideration that more than your path of least resistance is at stake. Unfortunately, too few people think like the boss and the boss is always right.

"Thinking outside of the box" is a phrase for challenging the status quo, or traditional techniques. My suggestion is to never get in the box. In the 1100s, we still believed that lead could be turned into gold. In the 1300s, we believed the earth was flat. In the 1800s, we believed manned flight was impossible. In the 1940s, we believed nuclear radiation was harmless. Plastic squeeze bottles of ketchup emerged 10 years after squeeze bottles of mustard when they sat side by side on every picnic table in America. Disposable cameras, fax machines, gutter guards, disposable diapers, birth control, the computer revolution, keeping the score on the upper left corner of the TV during the entire game, cell phones, voicemail, CD-players, remote controls, microwave ovens, intermittent windshield wipers ... The list goes on and on. The point is that you or I could have conceived any one of these ideas. We are in a period of history where we are challenging every aspect of our lives at a staggering rate. We are developing ways to live longer, healthier, more comfortable lives. Be a part of the revolution by not settling for how it is but how it could be. Add balance to your life by believing there is no limit on creativity. You just may become a part of history!

Merge your ideas with others. We, as humans, can be victims of our own biases. The "I'm right, you're wrong" mentality is easy to slip into. At least once a day, take a position of humility and find the expert in someone else. It is as easy asking someone's opinion and then listening. You will be out of the box in no time!

"The worst thing that can happen to you as an enthusiastic adult is that you could appear foolish to people who need to criticize. Let me assure you— enthusiasm is worth this risk. If you allow yourself to be enthusiastic, you will be so full of wonder; you will not care what people think."
- Barbara Sher, Author

Develop a passion. Add some new experiences to keep a touch of variety in your life. Same old, same old, is a great way to get old. Find at least one activity that fires you up, can completely absorb you, and is worth making a sacrifice. Engaging your brain in a passion is quite satisfying.

The three areas of our lives that require a balance plan are work, home, and stress relief. These areas must have the proper attention or we can become disoriented. Share your ideas for balancing these with your family and your employers for a well-rounded life that gives you the most satisfaction. Too much emphasis on work is a common problem that can lead to crisis in families and relationships. Your managers will question your commitment if you leave the office early for junior's soccer practice every day. Allowing the proper time for stress relief adds years to your life and keeps the wrinkles at bay. Balance these three aspects of your life by giving them all the proper attention and time that the people around you expect.

Financial balance will add years to your life. The Federal Reserve's most recent figures show revolving credit grew by 8.5 percent in November 1996. If you are in credit card debt, are afraid to answer the phone, are gradually needing more money each month to live, or do not have a written financial short or long-term plan, you are financially unbalanced. A number of recent student suicides have been linked to credit card debt. Money is not emotional. It is simple math. In Suze Orman's, *The 9 Steps to Financial Freedom*, financial freedom begins with the ability to understand your fear about money. If you have any of the above financial symptoms, call 1-800-501-SAVE (Consumer Counseling Credit Service) for a free evaluation of your finances and a plan to move forward. Get help if your finances have introduced stress into your home or business. You can beat financial imbalance.

If you do not have this type of financial stress in your life, consider yourself one of the lucky ones. Financial imbalance is a very common problem that can be devastating to your self-esteem, your family, and emotional balance.

There is also another type of financial imbalance. This imbalance concerns people who have worked so hard for their money that they do not enjoy spending it. This is the lesser of two evils but, nevertheless, a cause of stress. If you fall into this category, try Stephan Pollan's book, *Die Broke*, who says that your last check should be written to the funeral director, and it should bounce!

Slow down and enjoy Bethesda Country Club's 17th green. Bethesda, Maryland.

Remove the burden of spending money by remembering why you worked so hard to earn it. To enjoy it. From time to time, do not try to find the absolute, lowest price in town.

None of us are getting out alive, so budget some money to spend just for the enjoyment or to give to charity. You can make more. Give a small amount of money to a stranger who could use it. Money can't buy happiness? Tell me that after you give some away. If you get a windfall, a lucky run in Vegas, or an unexpected bonus, spend it on something (or someone) nice that you can associate with the good fortune. It is a great way to buy a memory. Financial habits can dissolve into personality habits. Be at peace with your finances.

"I'm a great believer in the benefits of a balanced, poised finish."
- Ernie Els, Professional Golfer

Slow, No Wake! Every decision that you make leaves a wake. That wake is part of your responsibility to those around you. Maintain balance by anticipating the ripple effects of your actions.

Expand your circle by communicating once a day with a person you have not contacted in a while. When you are traveling for business, take some personal time to ski, fish, or enjoy an activity that you cannot do at home. Pay extra attention to the people who love you. Stay balanced and you will be happier.

Without balance, a smooth, rhythmic, effective golf swing is impossible. Lacking balance in your golf swing is like driving on a flat tire. You can get there, but the ride is going to be rough. A loss of balance is usually the result of something else missing from your swing: an improper setup, take-away, or shoulder turn. Balance is what makes a good golf swing effortless. Without it, the best you will ever be is a chop.

Tempo controls your balance. The PGA players' tempo is a thing of beauty. All of them. Controlled tempo is a consistent feature of all good golf swings. Slow backswing, minimal unnecessary movement, and a synchronized motion. Complete symmetry is the key to awesome distance and explosive power with minimal effort. Efficiency and art.

Slow your swing to improve your balance. For some reason, a faster swing seems to give us more distance when actually it is just the opposite. A quick swing does not allow your weight to shift with the proper tempo, balance, and strength.

"Swing tempo has been the most important factor in my career. It relieves the pressure and stress of the game."
- Nick Faldo, Professional Golfer

To regain or improve balance, slow everything down and keep your knees bent and loose. Think about producing your swing at half the speed you normally do and try not to lock your legs in any one position. The big muscle groups should dominate the golf swing. Legs, back, and shoulders. Concentrate on rotating your hips and shoulders if you feel unbalanced. Most amateurs have a limited shoulder rotation. Turn, don't slide your shoulders and rotate your back to the target. The shoulder rotation is where power is generated. Lack of power is an indication of an improper shoulder rotation. Turn your left shoulder past your right foot to get all of your weight behind the ball and you will maximize distance.

"It's a compromise between what your ego wants you to do, what experience tells you to do, and what your nerves let you do."
- Bruce Crampton, Professional Golfer,
on balance in golf.

During full swings, there is a tendency to get your weight out on your toes and either fall forward or fall toward the target. Get your weight back to the center of your feet, or even a little bit on your heels, to counter for leaning forward and chasing the ball that's in front of you. Reduce unnecessary movements (this is what they mean by a compact swing). Keep your lower body firmly planted and finish your swing with a pose. Balance will bring length and power back into your game.

It is easy to detect when your balance is off. An indication of good balance is the ability to pose after each swing. If, at the end of your follow through, your weight is throwing you out of your setup stance, or you are not standing still after your shot, it's time to put balance back into your swing. It is a mistake that is very easy to correct.

 Stay balanced to get the most out of every shot.

14th Tee ➡

Rancho La Quinta's 6th. Bite off as much as you like. Palms Springs, California.

NUMBER 14 - GAMBLING AND RISK

"I made $215 - the $200 I figured I'd lose and the $15 I actually won."
- Ken Harrelson, Professional Baseball Player, on golf hustling.

All work and no risk makes Jack a dull boy! Adding risk to your life is a great way to get your heart pumping and truly feel alive. On this hole, you must decide whether to lay up or go for the green in two. During this two-down automatic Nassau we will venture into why risk and wealth go hand in hand. We will roll the dice in your comfort zone and speculate on techniques for using and understanding our gut instincts. I will tip my hand to show you the difference between gambling and risk and how an occasional gamble should not wipe you out. Grab the short straw in the next few pages for suggestions for financial success with an investment strategy that is the odds-on favorite. You will also learn the two most important questions in golf.

Risk - (risk) - the chance of injury, damage, or loss; dangerous chance; hazard. Two possible outcomes - loss or no loss.

Gam-ble - (gam' bul) - to play games of chance for money or some other stake, to take a risk in order to gain some advantage. Three possible outcomes - loss, no loss, or gain.

Risk tolerance. Gambling and risk can be your best friend or your worst nightmare. No one has an inherited risk tolerance that they are born with and destined to live with. Instead, risk tolerance is like a muscle. It can be developed with knowledge, experience, and practice. Great business minds understand risk and the role emotions play when making decisions. These minds always quantify as much as they can with numbers. After the numbers have been evaluated, what happens next is largely dependent on our minds or emotions or gut instincts. Do not ignore your emotions. These gut feelings have significant value, but only after you have done your homework. How confident you become before pulling the trigger is completely dependent on your risk tolerance.

Try to **mix facts and emotions like a mixed drink**. Too many facts (mixer) will not ruin the drink, but too much emotion (alcohol) can ruin the drink and your evening. When making business decisions, just a shot of emotion, please.

Those who can assess risk with the most accuracy make the best business decisions. Reduce your fear of the unknown when assessing risk by conducting extensive research to create accurate projections of pros, cons, and alternatives. Risk evaluation has certainly found its way into the boardroom. The '80s introduced the CIO, or Chief Information Officer. The '90s introduced the CRO, or Chief Risk Officer. These executives keep their corporations out of hot water concerning exposure to government regulations, susceptibility to hackers, recalls, and other liability exposure. Managing risk can be a full-time job.

Getting paid last is the key to wealth. In business, the last person to get paid carries the most risk and therefore has the most control. It is why owners make more than employees and why some millionaires go broke. If you are not the recipient of what is left over after everything is said and done, someone is, justifiably, making more money than you are. The wealthiest people are comfortable with the risk of getting paid last.

"I'm working as hard as I can to get my life and my cash to run out at the same time. If I can just die after lunch Tuesday, everything will be perfect."
- Doug Sanders, Professional Golfer,
Senior PGA Tour player

Sometimes a risk strategy has to be altered. Change your strategy when your goals are not being met or the likelihood of their success has changed from probable to improbable. Maybe you have researched improperly or an outside influence has entered the picture - a competitor sets up shop across the street or a major account goes out of business. The most common mistake is that you need more cash than you thought. Do not throw in the towel too early, but be ready to make changes quickly. What you evaluated yesterday may be different today.

CONDITION

Managing your financial assets is an exercise in successfully dealing with risk. Maximizing returns while minimizing risk is every investor's dream. So how do you find that perfect combination of risk and reward?

Success with your money is no different from success in any endeavor. It requires patience, an open mind, hard work, time, and guidance from outside resources. I have combined a few of the Eighteen Holes of Success *with a four-step process created by Salomon Smith Barney's Consulting Group for your financial success.*

Hole Number two, **What's Your Target?**, *taught us that success is impossible without a clear definition of a specific goal. The first step begins by* **Setting Your Financial Objectives**. *This can be difficult because most of us are experts at something other than financial management. Start by looking at major financial events that are inevitable and evaluate your desired lifestyle. If you need guidance, professional financial consultants can help you understand the myriad of financial options available to you and ensure that your financial needs for retirement, future college expenses, major purchases, or other personal financial goals are met.*

The last hole we played, **Balance***, is one hole that you will certainly want to include in your financial strategy as you* **Develop Your Asset Allocation Strategy***. Your objective here is to*

.13 12.13 ▲ TXN -3.88 60 ▼ F +0.1 36.52▲ AOL +0.60 58.59▲

APL +.56 57.65 ▲ NWSL -0.24 65.24 ▼ MTCH -0.25 10.69 ▼ EBAY

diversify your portfolio to maximize returns while minimizing exposure to loss. Allocation strategies can range from very conservative to very aggressive. Asset allocation should include a review of trends and developments in the capital markets, an analysis of international economies, your current asset allocation, and your objectives and time horizon.

*The third step combines concepts from Hole Number ten, **The Leader Board** and Hole Number eleven, **Know Your Partner** and involves the process of **Selecting Investment Managers**. Your objective here is to choose a variety of managers that are worthy of a long-term partnership. Independent analysis and evaluation of the various professional investment managers must be done before selections can be made. Companies that only recommend their financial products or services are not offering you the appropriate number of options for financial success.*

*The final step is to **Monitor Performance**. Success cannot be achieved without periodic review of your portfolio's performance, the activities of your investment managers, and the attainment of your financial goals. Periodic, independent review of your selected investment managers ensures that they meet the industry's highest levels of quality and performance for your financial success.*

These strategies will minimize your risk and increase the likelihood that you will reach your objectives.

In some cases, throwing in the towel is exactly what you should do (Some hints for this are on the next hole, Fore!). Determine specifically where that point is well before you get there. Pick a dollar value or a timetable (or both) where you should cut your losses and get out. Just because you think an idea or investment will work does not mean it will. **Determine <u>beforehand</u> exactly how much you are willing to lose before you dig a hole that is too deep to jump out of.**

Risk is slightly different from gambling. Gambling involves a game of chance, where the odds of success are difficult to predict or are less than or equal to 50%. Consistent gambling is a loser, but occasional gambles may pay off. This is where gut instinct can give you an edge. Most of your entrepreneurs have a stomach for gambling. Know the difference between taking a good risk and staying away from a bad bet.

One way to help you define your risk exposure is to determine specifically all of the "upside" and "downside." The term, "upside" is all of the good that comes from any situation and all of the reasons why you should do something. The opposite of "upside" is "downside." "Downside" is all of the bad that comes from any situation and the reasons why you wouldn't do something because of the risks or potential negative results. Upside is more. More money, more freedom, more happiness, more time. Downside is less. Less time, less money, less freedom. Avoiding downside is more important than finding all of the upside.

Emotional risk. Up to this point, we have only discussed risk as it pertains to business decisions. There are risks associated with life that do not involve your money. You may want to perform on stage or change careers. At some point we have all dreamed about that perfect life that seems to be reserved for others. We only regret what we do not try. Children do not have the monopoly on dreams, laughter, or raw belief!

Risk is personal. Everyone has his or her own tolerance. A risk will never be a sure thing. Adding some risk into your life will expand your comfort zone. The capability to properly evaluate risk is a valuable skill that too few possess. If all you are expending is energy and the gamble does not pan out, then all you have lost is time. Fortunately, the man who made time made plenty of it.

> *"I can tell right away if a guy is a winner or a loser just by the way he conducts himself on the golf course."*
>
> *- Donald Trump, Real Estate Developer and Casino Owner*

Gambling and evaluating risk on the golf course is similar to what we do in business, but it is more fun and you have less to lose.

Course management is the proper assessment of risk and a valuable club to keep in the bag. Jack Nicklaus has written entire books on the topic of course management. It is critical to achieving success with your golf. Mental errors are every bit as costly as poor swings. Using your strengths and mentally admitting your weaknesses will help you stay in control. Poor course management can get you into unnecessary trouble. Golf is so much like billiards because you don't merely play one shot at a time, you are thinking about positioning for your next shot. A good "leave" is critical.

Risk on the golf course is something you should evaluate before every shot. It's the answer to the question, "Where don't I want to be?" Not knowing the risk of an errant shot can cost you strokes. A 100-yard shot may be easier than a 40-yard shot. Punching out from a bad lie is usually going to cost you less strokes than trying to reach the green.

Jail, on the golf course (and in life) is the result of miscalculating risk. Fortunately, the jail cell created by the afternoon sun on Canyon Gate Country Club's 14th, like everything in Vegas, is merely a mirage. Las Vegas, Nevada.

Play **defense** with your **club selection** and alignment. Think **offense during the swing** or shot. This means if there is trouble in front of the green, take an extra club and align yourself with the safe part of the green. When you are over the shot, swing aggressively and confidently. You have already accounted for the risk with your club selection and alignment.

Keep the ball in play. If you want to lower your scores dramatically, play the round with one ball. Play like the ball you are playing with is the last one on earth. Protect it, hit it straight, and do not lose it. Penalties from lost balls and hazards usually turn into a 2-stroke penalty, and sometimes more if you count the loss of rhythm. Not losing a ball makes carding worse than bogey difficult. If you have never broken 85, keep every club in the trunk except your four iron through sand wedge (and putter) and you will break 85 the next time out.

Wagering. Most golfers enjoy a wager on the golf course. A friendly bet can do wonders for your concentration. However, it can also add some pressure. My best advice is to pick an amount that you do not mind losing, and make your bets based on that. No one can enjoy losing an uncomfortable amount of money, so do not bet until you have that figure in mind. And nobody cares if you want only a small wager or do not feel comfortable gambling at all. If they do, maybe a friendly bet is not what they have in mind.

Only gamble small amounts with new acquaintances. Losing a substantial amount of money can put a wedge between the best of friends. It can also kill a potential friendship. I rarely gamble with people that I am meeting for the first time on the golf course. It is a difficult situation. If you win, maybe the strokes were not set properly. You can look like a liar if you shoot your career round. That holds for your opponent as well. My advice is to gamble only with people you have played with before and only an amount that everyone is willing to comfortably lose. I can play for $10 a hole while my brother hyperventilates in that environment. Determine your gambling comfort level first.

The more important the round, the more conservative you should be. It all depends on where your strengths lie. The two most important questions in golf are "How much am I comfortable losing?" and "Where don't I want to be?" As long as you ask yourself those questions, you will be comfortable with the risks you are taking on the course.

"Most people would rather be certain they're miserable, than risk being happy."
- Robert Anthony, Author

15th Tee

"Hit a house!" is more than an expression on Fieldstone Country Club's 12th and 14th shared real estate. Wilmington, Delaware.

NUMBER 15 - LAYUP

"Genius is eternal patience."
- Michelangelo, sculptor, artist, architect,
and poet of the sixteenth century

The "business lay-up" is standard procedure for the pros. This short hole is reachable in two, however, the green is surrounded by water. In the next few pages you will see how doing less may get you more. No need for your driver, a smooth 5-iron and you will learn how to appear more intelligent and project more confidence than you do right now. I will teach you why saying nothing is actually saying quite a bit, and in many cases the best strategy. The power of patience is the heart of the lay-up!

Patience. We all have a tendency to be quick to speak or answer a question. Whoa, there cowboy. You do not get points for the speed with which you make a statement. We naturally think that the first one on the buzzer gets the prize. Jeopardy - yes, business - no. The last one to speak has all the power. Every <u>Sales 101</u> class closes with, "ask for the business, and then be quiet! The next person to speak loses." During business communication the rookies jump to a response, as a show of intelligence or wit when pausing, thinking, and then responding makes the best impression and communicates the most intelligent thought.

Silence is pure defense. The old saying, "Say nothing and let them think you are dense or open your mouth and prove it," is very true. I guarantee no damage can be done during silence. I know you can think of at least five instances where you said something you regretted, in the interest of humor, getting ahead, or as an attempt to impress. Shhhh!

The most important business lay-up, my friend, is to **think before you talk**! You have two ears and one mouth so listen twice as much as you talk. In sales, avoid the "show up and throw up" or "spray and pray" sales call. Silence is a lay-up.

When you are not talking there are two things you should be doing.

The first is to manage your facial expressions and body language. A poker face is a valuable asset. Hide your emotions until you get all of the facts. Try to always have a calm, confident look, and give a gentle nod from time to time to the speaker. You will always look as if you understand what is going on, and that whoever is speaking is making sense. Whether they are is not your problem.

And, just because you look like you understand everything going on around you does not mean you do. You have not committed to anything; you'll just look smarter.

*The second thing you should be doing when you are not talking is listening. To listen is to learn, and you cannot learn when you are talking. There are two ways that most of us listen. The first is when you are not talking but you are thinking about what you are going to say or do next. This is not listening. It is talking **very quietly** to yourself and what most of us do. It is why in almost every meeting someone asks a question that was answered two minutes ago. The second is actually listening. When you listen your brain has to be focused on learning and processing what is being said. Know the difference and listen more.*

> *"Nothing is often a good thing to say, and always a clever thing to say."*
> *-Will Durant, American Historian and Philosopher*

Before you make a phone call, plan for a minute what you are going to say. Ask yourself if you should leave a voicemail or not, and the consequences it may have. Also, now don't pass out; be prepared for the person to actually answer the phone. In some primitive cultures it happens from time to time. Be to the point, and conclude with a specific action or action plan. A touch of humor is always well received. Get into the habit of planning your phone conversation and thinking before you speak.

Use all the time you have. Another strategic lay-up technique of the all-stars is they **do not stroke the check until the absolute last minute**! You will make better decisions. Don't offer that employee a job, don't make that purchase, don't make any commitments, until you have done your research. Check references for everyone you are about to do business with. Employees, contractors, and baby-sitters. The amount of time it takes for you to check references, and check them thoroughly, is a small percentage based on the damage a stranger can do.

One of the worst feelings I have ever experienced was when I made a substantial equipment purchase for computer equipment early in my business. The order was for $10,000 worth of equipment and I was itching to spend the money. Why? I do not know. I left a check for the entire amount because we needed it in a hurry. I checked on the order a day later and that familiar phone company sound, "doo-doo-doo, the number you have dialed has been disconnected and you are a complete idiot for leaving a check for the whole amount..." The first "doo" was all I needed to hear. **That's two OB.** *They had my money and I had a worthless receipt. Frantic, I went to my partner and explained the situation. We put a stop on the check, but it was too late. The bank had already cashed it.* **Nice three jack.** *I drove to the suppliers business and the place looked condemned, padlocks everywhere, and nothing but tape on the windows.* **Put me down for an X.** *Devastation. I had just spent our last $10,000 putting myself on the bottom of a creditors list. I've invested better. I had the salesperson's card and found her home number. I left a message and waited.*

Checking every option of tracking this company down was an exercise in depression. That afternoon the phone rang and it was the salesperson. She said they had merged with another company and had just completed the move and she wanted to give me the new number and address! I have not prepaid for anything since that day!

"In the business world, everyone is paid in two coins: cash and experience. Take the experience first; the cash will come later."
        - Anonymous

Sleep on it. Patience when evaluating new ideas or strategic directions is invaluable. Tomorrow, today's good idea is a great idea. The day after, it gets even better. Any highly emotional situation can be clarified with one night's rest. Avoid jumping to conclusions. Tomorrow, you will see today's problems more clearly. Back off ideas that lose momentum. Saying "No" too often has never sent anyone to the poorhouse.

Recognize the power of positioning and that long-term business is like a chess game. If an objective cannot be accomplished now, position yourself for the future. Look at a lost sale as a delayed sale. Keep the prospect alive and the bridge intact. Persistency coupled with strategic positioning over time will eventually bring home the deal. Life is long and a sales cycle can be longer. A good friend of mine taught me that, "No - means Nooooo Problem!"

New ideas can be ahead of their time. When your new ideas are shot down, end the battle before taking your ball and going home. The world will fight change, often violently. Gradually ease new ideas into the minds of the cynics.

Make sure you take the lay-up shot in business. Check references and evaluate vendors. Incorporate some patience into your career, and you will make better decisions and learn more. You do not have to hit a three-wood when a seven-iron will do.

You have not won it until you have won it. This is the best lesson that golf continues to reinforce, and one that I religiously apply to my business affairs. How may times have you been standing in the fairway thinking birdie when your opponent is dropping next to the lake 30 yards in front of the tee. You have him 2 down with three to play. He is toast. So, of course, he bounces one off a sprinkler head and hits one 240 yards when his longest shot all day was 190. Three footer for par. It burrows into your head so deep that you pull yours left, splash your third shot out of the bunker long, and miss the four-footer. Par beats bogey. You lose. One up with two to play. Never, ever, ever, count it until it's over.

Losing a deal to unknown competition, hostile takeovers, and your good contact getting promoted are reasons a deal can go from in the bag to in the can in ten seconds. Be prepared.

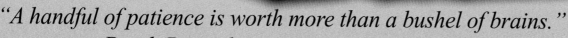

The biggest waste in golf is forgetting the strength of the lay-up shot. The most common is the second shot on par fives. Why do golfers who have never hit the ball over 220 yards take a 3 wood when they are 260 yards from the green? What is that? Please stop today.

"A handful of patience is worth more than a bushel of brains."
- Dutch Proverb

A 100- to 120-yard shot is the easiest shot in golf. If you are 260 yards from the green, hit a 7-iron 150 yards and you have the easiest shot in golf left. **In anybody's world, par is still a great score.** You have eliminated a major catastrophe with the 3-wood (if you butcher the 7-iron, you would have certainly butchered the 3-wood, and you are not as deep in the woods) and now can confidently hit the next shot because, dig this, you are actually managing your game.

The hardest game in the world just got easier. Add the confidence of hitting a smart, well-planned shot, and you have taken a par five and turned it into a 110-yard par 3. What a birdie opportunity, and an easy par. Even if you chose the three wood and hit it well, you still have a 30 or 40 yard shot which can be tougher than a 100 yard shot.

The lay-up shot is what is meant by course management. Focusing on course management will lower your score more than you think. The move from scoring in the 90s to the 80s is mostly through course management.

 Bogeys are fine - Doubles are killers.

 Attempting the "I can hook it around that tree and keep it under that second branch and feather it through those traps up to the green 190 yards away" shot can completely kill the round.

 Don't follow a bad shot with a stupid shot.

In certain cases, choosing not to lay-up is OK. The high-risk option can be more fun and give you more satisfaction (if you actually pull it off), but be prepared for it to drain momentum and confidence.

Position the ball on as many holes as possible for the same shot. For instance, aim for a 150-yard approach shot on par fours. Even if you can get the ball to the 130-yard marker, club down to leave a 150-yard shot. Hitting all of your approach shots from 150 yards will add confidence and let you groove your swing from that distance.

On your next round, on all four par fives, plan your approach shot to be from your most comfortable distance. If you hit 4 shots from your most comfortable distance, you should have 3 or 4 birdie putts.

When laying up in front of a lake, do not try to get too close to the water. Select the club that has no chance of getting there. Like they say, "when laying up, uh, lay-up."

The lay-up mentality also includes the "easy punch out" from the woods after a bad shot. After a poor drive, punch out and the likelihood of making bogey is almost guaranteed. Saving par after a bad shot is one of the best feelings in golf. It puts you back in control.

A risky shot with a branch in your way? A 200-yard carry over water? Hit it 60 yards with a five-iron, under the branch, take your wedge and put it on the green and make the putt. Worst case, bogey. The alternative is dropping in three, hitting your fourth shot, and you're looking at double or worse. Not to mention having to deal with that new burning sensation in your chest.

Remember that straight is better than long. If you want to shoot in the low 80s, you can bogey half the holes. That's not bad considering that if all you tried to do was bogey every hole, you probably could. When "laying up" off the tee, aim for the "fat" or safe part of the fairway away from the OB stakes or water. Do not be afraid to play for bogey. It is a powerful way to play the golf course.

Always aim for the center of the green. Aiming at flags can lead to double quicker than you think. Aiming for the center gives you more room for error. If you play for the center and the pin is left, you can pull it a bit and find yourself tight. You don't have to tell your playing partners that you pulled it, let them think you're that good. For club selection, always use the distance to the center of the green and you will putt sooner.

Keep your game in control by playing high percentage shots. Poor play is usually just as many bad decisions as it is bad swings. When on the tee of a 330-yard hole, there is absolutely no upside in hitting the driver. Unless you can hit a driver straight and 330 yards. In that case, you would have a sponsor, which you don't. So take out your 3-iron and keep it in play.

16th Tee ➡

The crocodiles protecting the 13th green on the Lost City Golf Course give a new meaning to the term "hazard." Sun City, South Africa.

NUMBER 16 - FORE!

It is a shame there's no word used in business like "Fore" is used on the golf course. If there were, I'm sure it would be another four-letter word or a couple of them.

"More people would learn from their mistakes if they weren't so busy denying that they made them."
- Anonymous

This hole may look familiar because it has a tee shot like <u>Lay-up</u> and an approach shot like <u>Calm</u>. The only difference is that the swimming pool is about 200 yards just off the right side of the fairway, hence the name. Let's face it, mistakes are part of the program. This hole will teach you how to minimize the damage of those inevitable mistakes and how and when to deliver the message. If you stay on the cart path here you won't miss the signs telling you when you have maximized a situation. A secondary goal, of course, is not to kill any of the swimmers. "Fore, right!"

Expect problems. Going down with the ship is out of fashion. Getting everyone off the ship, including yourself, is more in vogue. When it hits the fan, be ready. It is going to happen when you least expect it. This comes in the form of losing a big sale, losing an essential employee, or one of your clients missing a big payment. The point is that the ship is sinking, so be prepared to yell "Fore!" and be prepared to yell it loudly.

Report bad news early. A major catastrophe usually starts out as a minor one. The sooner people know, the sooner everyone can respond, and the sooner you can get to a solution. People at the top need to know bad news as early as possible. Hiding bad news to conceal your faults will eventually be a fault added to the list. If you screw up, communicate and move on. You will do less damage and upper management will appreciate the heads-up and your confidence. However, consistently reporting bad news will get you noticed for the wrong reasons.

"Mr. Corleone is a man who insists on hearing bad news immediately!"
THE WALL STREET JOURNAL.
-Robert Duvall as Tom in "The Godfather."

ofit **Page B4.**

Forecast the potential storm. If there is a remote possibility that a disaster may strike, let everyone know. If it never hits, so what? If it hits and you could have sounded the alarm, I'd hate to be you. Use your judgment and forecast storms, not light rain showers. Crying wolf or being melodramatic when it is not necessary can waste energy and limit your credibility.

When the storm hits. The objective here is to minimize the damage caused by making bad decisions. Magnifying faults of others is a waste of time that is nowhere on the repair work order.

Focus only on an immediate solution to the situation. If the problem is cash flow, visit your creditors and your bank(s). Tell them the situation and ask for help. When the problem may influence your clients' businesses, telling them immediately is not soon enough. A quick way to lose customers is to sit on information that's going to cost them money. You will have a repeat customer if you take this advice. The longer you wait, the more trouble you are going to cause.

Do not use "Fore" when "Calm" will work. In these cases, whispering "Fore" is the best course of action. Every deal has two sides. When to "get in" and when to "get out." When to "get out" never seems to get as much press as when to "get in" does. When to "get out" is a cornerstone of the "Fore!" message. When your job becomes an unbearable burden, whisper "Fore!" When you have climbed four steps on the corporate ladder and the top two steps are not going to be vacant in your lifetime, whisper "Fore!" and quietly make a move. If you'll never be able to match this year's salary, it may be time to whisper "Fore!" If your quality of life is suffering because of your relationship(s) at home, whisper "Fore!" Do not be lulled into complacency! Recognize when your satisfaction is being compromised and quickly and quietly chart a new course. If you desire a new career, prepare to leave. If your personal life is stale, prepare to communicate. There are a variety of glass ceilings that we encounter on our way to success. They are called glass ceilings because they are very difficult to see. Plan your exits as carefully as your entrances.

As you are aware, I have quite a bit of respect for my business partner, Charlie. During our time together, when the phone would ring and the call was for me, it was **usually** *a client telling me why he or she could not buy our software. When it was for Charlie, it was* **always** *a client telling him that something was wrong with our software. When was the last time that you contacted your software manufacturer when something worked great? After four years of that, Chaz had had enough. Not that he had a problem with the calls, he understood that this was a necessary part of the process, but he also knew it would never change.*

That fact, coupled with his dream of making movies, pushed him to Hollywood (now affectionately known as Charlie-wood). We worked out a transition plan so I could make the business work without him. I always knew I would lose him to the Big Silver. The man whispered "Fore" and split. He stayed as long as he could, but his day had become a burden. He recognized it and never looked back. I had to call him from time to time and yell "Fore!" concerning his payments. But the company survived.

Running the company by myself had a certain hollow feeling. A few years later, I whispered "Fore" and split. I was not interested in taking the business to the next level. I recognized it and never looked back. Fortunately, there was someone who was. The new owner had to call from time to time and yell "Fore!" concerning his payments. But the company survived.

Know when you've won or lost. Cutting losses or being comfortable with gains is one way to yell "Fore!" Determine your parameters for what constitutes a moderate loss and a moderate gain and live within those parameters. What we are trying to avoid is a significant loss. Know exactly where a **moderate** loss turns into a **significant** loss and get out of the cart at that point. We all know someone who stayed in too long and got buried. After a great return on a stock, click "Fore!" to your (discount) broker and sell.

Have a backup plan. Having an appropriate backup plan will significantly reduce how often you shout "Fore!" Murphy's Law states that things are only allowed to screw up when you do not have a backup plan. Have copies of important files, and prepare for the power to go off at exactly the wrong time. During presentations with your computer, have backup transparencies for the "CRITICAL ERROR: 200 CLIENTS ARE IN THE ROOM" error message that technical support has never seen before. Check your insurance policies every year, maintain a savings account, and have a good spare tire.

In golf, your game doesn't just check out, it burns the hotel down.

There are more ways than one to yell "Fore!" concerning your golf game. I do not mean specifically yelling "Fore!" to avoid injuring another golfer (or swimmer). I'm talking about when you have completely lost your ability to play at your normal skill level. Golf is the only sport that is cruel enough to give and take without letting you know. I play a little basketball. Some nights I'm on and some nights I'm a little bit off. Fortunately, basketball players don't go through periods where they throw the ball over the backboard or shoot airballs that miss by 15 feet. Only in the cruel world of golf does that happen.

When this happens, just let it go. It is bigger than you are. Don't play for a few weeks. You won't forget everything you learned if you take a week or two off. So what if you do? The hotel's on fire anyway, remember.

"Well, sir, I'd recommend the 4:05 train."
- Harry Vardon's caddy, after Vardon asked him,
"What should I take here?"

Fore!

Inside 100 Yards. Working on your short game is the quickest improvement you can make. You may be hitting it sideways, but if you can scramble for bogey or par, at least you can score. The short game can bleed life into the rest of your bag.

Simplify your game. Keep your eye on the ball a little longer, follow through a little further, and swing slower. Simplify. Take a lesson if you are way out of line. Do anything that may add to your confidence.

"I needed 'em both."
- Bob Lanier, basketball player, on playing in a threesome with a doctor and a priest.

Count jokes, not strokes. Play only to have fun. Expect to shoot a new career worst and don't worry about it. Just get back to enjoying it. Even the pros struggle. It is part of the game. Don't let your frustration add to the problem.

The area of the game that is the most fun is the long game; tee shots, long irons, and iron shots. Focus on making solid contact and forget about where it lands and your score. The long game can bring some fun back into it for you. Try to maintain a positive outlook about your swing and your game. Focus on hitting it straight, not long. It is OK to yell "Fore!" about your game. Everybody goes through slumps in the game of golf. It's an unfortunate part of the game, but if you are prepared, you may shorten the nightmare.

That's not the smoke alarm I hear in the background is it?

17th Tee ➡

Fore!

The Atlantic Ocean and Table Bay Mountain are pleasant backdrops for almost every hole at Milnerton Golf Club. Cape Town, South Africa.

NUMBER 17 - NICE GUYS FINISH FIRST

The world has changed. It used to be "Nice guys finish last" but no more. Being nice does not get enough credit for the return on investment. Nothing has helped me more in business than just being nice.

This hole is the only hole your group will remember when they talk about who they played with today. Now that you are fully into the groove of your round, the 17th hole is a great time for a momentum check. Your objective now is to avoid doing anything foolish that could diminish an otherwise perfect round.

Losing your pleasant disposition is like triple bogeying 17. It is all anybody will remember. On this hole I will show you how your routine errands can become anticipated events. We will open your new bank account with an unlimited currency of compliments and generosity that crushes the return on any other investment you will ever make. It's completely tax free, and the more you spend, the more you have. I will also give you some tips on getting in good with the golf gods. Nice people get it all.

Being nice to people is a more enjoyable way to spend the day. It consists of a consistent pleasant demeanor, a helpful attitude, a smile, and a gentle sense of humor. People have a tendency to trust you if you are nice.

Give out genuine compliments. Compliments are free and they feel good to everybody. How many compliments do you get in any given week? If you are like most of us, not many. Find reasons to give genuine compliments. A compliment is a simple, pure gesture you can make to anyone, at any time, and get an instant positive feeling about yourself. The compliment dynamic is powerful medicine.

Every person in the world who wakes up and gets to work spends some amount of time getting ready, selecting clothes, and generally preparing themselves for their day. Women have additional jewelry, hair, nail, and other decisions that men do not have to make. Nevertheless, we all spend at least 30 minutes preparing ourselves. The point is that with all of those decisions made in the morning, at least one of them will be the right one. Find that one and mention it. Nice tie. You look great today, have you been on vacation? What a great necklace. What a cool watch, where did you get it? Got it? It brightens everyone's day. Yours included. On those rare occasions where you do not feel like talking, make direct eye contact and smile. Being nice is drawing attention to the little things that usually go unnoticed.

*This is how you can turn your daily activities into meaningful experiences. Compliment the checkout person at the grocery store and at the dry cleaner. Compliment your mechanic. Soon you will develop a relationship and you will **both** look forward to your next visit. We all appreciate being noticed.*

The nicer you are, the better you feel. A person cannot be too generous or do too much for others. Be generous with your time, your money, and your material possessions. The difference between being cheap and being generous is only a few dollars. Your spending habits can become a part of your personality. Your financial well-being has nothing to do with it. Generosity comes from the heart. Cheap people have stingy personalities and do not forgive others easily. Give as much as you can. You will always get more than you give.

"The art of dealing with people is the foremost secret of successful men. A man's success in handling people is the very yardstick by which the outcome of his whole life's work is measured."
- Paul Packer, Author

Keep foul language to a minimum. You will be guaranteed not to offend anyone. You will never find yourself in any situation where being polite and PG-rated will not help you.

Defend the absent party. We have all been put in the awkward position of participating in a conversation where a person not in attendance is being insulted or disparaged. Don't participate in the witch-hunt. Be the cool side of the pillow, and say something nice about the victim. This accomplishes three things. One, it makes it difficult for the pettiness to continue; two, it reduces the likelihood of you ever being the target; and three, it gently reminds the children to play fair.

Care what other people think about you. The person who says, "I don't care what anybody else thinks" may not know what they are missing. It is an expensive attitude. Quite a bit is determined when you are not around, and we have enough problems without giving others more reasons to knock us down. Do not give your employer another reason to let you go. If you are guilty of not caring what others think, you are being defensive. I suggest conducting your affairs as if you do care what others think.

*In 1985, John F. Akers was selected as Chairman of IBM. I started working full-time for IBM in 1987. To educate myself about the company, I researched, among other things, the Board of Directors, CEO, and Division Heads just in case there was a pop quiz. One of the articles I found was written by Mr. Akers himself. It was titled, How I became CEO. I thought, "This could be good." The article was one page and said that he became CEO because he was **nice** to everyone. His customers, service reps, manufacturing managers, line employees, staff employees, temporary employees, and everyone in between. And that was it. I turned the page over as if I did not have the whole article. I did. Hmmm. This guy got to be CEO of the largest computer corporation in the world by being nice. Note to self. Not talent, hard work, luck, strategic planning, or anything else. He said he got there because he was nice.*

*He was ousted, of course, in 1993 when IBM posted its largest losses in company history. Nevertheless, the man steered the ship we would all love to steer. **Nice** can get you there, but then its up to you.*

Have a personal goal for what you want people to think of you. That does not mean you have to be a pushover to be nice. You can state your ideas or positions plainly, with a smile, and with concern for everyone's feelings. If you have an issue with someone, take the issue directly to him or her. In many cases, you will find you may not have the whole story. If you do, it is a good time to, calmly and confidentially clear the air.

Remember Names. "I'm bad with names" is the coward's way of saying; "I don't care." Brush up on your name skills by simply paying attention during introductions. It takes concentration, but do it. "We've met before but I can't remember your name" is less awkward than the timid alternative of saying nothing. In addition, if someone clearly has forgotten your name, go easy on him or her by offering a hand and saying your name (first and last) out loud. To which they will respond with gratitude, "Sure, (your first name here), how are you."

Being nice is one of the first things that I remember learning as a child. I am afraid it has become a forgotten tool in the business community. Try to have a plan for what you'd like people to say about you; know that you'll gain more trust from people if you're nice; and when handling negative situations, try to frame your language as a form of guidance or advice. Compliment people as often as you can, and for a touch of class, compliment them in writing. Nice Guys do finish first.

Here are some sure winners to being a welcome member of any foursome.

Play at an even pace. Slow golfers bug everybody. Be prepared to hit your shot when it is your turn.

Act a little bit more like a caddie for the group. It is a sign of respect. If you are close to a rake and a player has just hit a shot out of the bunker, rake the bunker for them. I love it when people do that for me.

Be the last person in the foursome looking for someone else's ball. It shows a helpful spirit and does not hurt your relationship with the golf gods. Make sure you look as long or longer for their ball than they do. When I am having a tough day, muddy and bleeding, it helps my attitude immensely when my playing partners are helping me find my eggs.

Try to be the most liked in your foursome. Fix everybody's ball marks, not only your own. Everyone appreciates keeping the greens in shape. Do not be afraid to hustle and retrieve a club that someone forgot. Run back to the cart for them. If you are playing with older players, help them as much as you can. Show your foursome respect. Fix extra divots on the course, and if you see any trash on the golf course, pick it up. Trust me, your foursome will look up to you. You will also be one of the first people they call the next time they play.

Stand out of the way. Gary Player suggests standing opposite players' belly button (either in front of or directly behind). You will always be out of the player's peripheral vision if you follow this rule.

Say "play well" or "good luck" to your group on the first tee. This sets the tone for a friendly, challenging match. Also, shake hands with each member of your group on the 18th green. Caddies included.

I **strongly** recommend that you have a brief conversation with the Head Pro and assistants at any golf course you play. Good things seem to come from those brief conversations.

Most golf courses have a snack cart that will circle the course. Buy the first round. Everybody will probably end up picking up a round or two anyway. He who buys first is always the crowd favorite.

Do these things when you are playing with people for the first time. It gives a great first impression. Respect the golf course and help your playing partners as much as you can.

"Be nice to your kids. They'll choose your nursing home."
- Bumper Sticker

18th Tee ➡

The tropical climate of the Great Barrier Reef keeps Paradise Palms Country Club green year-round. Cairns, Australia.

NUMBER 18 - HONESTY

"I used to play golf with a guy who cheated so badly that he once had a hole in one and wrote down zero on his score card."
- Bob Bruce, Senior PGA Tour Golfer

This hole has a two-tiered purpose. First, to enlighten you to the power of honesty and, second, to open your eyes to the potential devastation of dishonesty. We'll take a cart ride through honesty with finances, how you can comfortably fight the urge to stretch the truth, and how being truthful with clients will win them over for life. And, hopefully, by the end of this chapter, you will never cheat on the golf course again.

Honesty in the office can make you rich. Make one promise to yourself, that you will never lie… to a customer, to a coworker, to anyone. It is the best investment you will ever make. The truth is easy to remember, and you will never flinch when someone asks you what you did last night. The actual facts are not as bad as your mind might let you think.

Make better decisions. The easiest way to guarantee your trustworthiness is to make decisions that make telling the truth easy. The truth is always the reasonable result of a reasonable situation. If you are lying, you are doing something wrong besides lying. You are failing somewhere else. The act of lying is the second failure. Fix the basic problem before you tell a lie to cover your tracks.

Once you tell a lie, you have lies to cover up. The cycle will never end. Even the appearance of dishonesty should be avoided at all costs. The truth is here and gone while deception never completely goes away. A lie is a time bomb waiting to explode because it can be exposed at any time in the future. Honesty brings peace of mind.

Being honest is less stressful and easier than the alternative. Dishonesty will gradually pilfer your character and will slowly become your most expensive, self-destructive habit. If you are honest, you will gain more trust, you will get more business, people will like you more, and they will want to be around you more. If you are a straight shooter, this chapter is not a big deal. However, if you have not seen the value of honesty, use these reasons to make it a priority, and you will.

The last person you deceive will be the next person that you need a favor from. It happens every time. Make it your philosophy not to burn anybody, and the next person you need a favor from is always going to say yes. Burning a bridge is an unrecoverable mistake. If that is all you get from this book, it is worth the pages you had to hump through to get here. This world is small, and it is only getting smaller. There are people that know of you through a friend of a friend of a friend. Get my drift? If you are not careful, enemies can be made without your knowledge.

It is easy to lie to a liar. Honest people are difficult to deceive because their character commands respect. However, deception among thieves is common. Tell the truth and you will impose your integrity on those around you.

Always negotiate in good faith. The basis for all successful negotiations is truth. Fair negotiations require two honest parties for the transaction to generate an environment for future transactions. Do not play games in negotiations. It only wastes time. Simply determine how far you are willing to go and actually draw the line there. Be patient and walk away when the offer crosses your line.

"Trickery and treachery are the practices of fools
that have not wits enough to be honest."
- Benjamin Franklin, American Statesman

The way you handle money is a window into your personality. Do not spend more than you have and always pay bills on time. Do not make people ask you for money. Asking for money is awkward and unpleasant. Do not put a generous person through it. A cash loan or flexible payment terms is a courtesy to you. Do not view your payment as a favor, it is the other half of the deal. Your creditor has done you the favor.

Family Loans. Borrowing money from family should be taken very seriously. Do not expect them to look the other way. Pay them back under the terms you agreed to, and treat the situation as a formal business transaction. It's good for your business discipline, and you may need their help in the future. Blood is thicker than water, but money is thicker than blood. A family loan that is paid back will secure a future loan and enhance your relationship.

In the event that you cannot pay a bill, call the creditor and tell them when they will receive your payment. If you must request a special payment schedule, do it. Any creditor, or friend for that matter, will accept a payment schedule as opposed to not getting paid at all.

In social situations, pay for your drinks, dinner, and more than your share of the tip or get comfortable eating and drinking alone. If you gamble, pay your bets.

Do not fudge your expense account. Is $24.32 worth your job?

I have found that being honest is the best technique I can use. Right up front, tell people what you're trying to accomplish and what you're willing to sacrifice to accomplish it."
-Lee Iacocca, Chairman, Chrysler Corporation

I made the mistake of receiving a questionable payment from a customer and not notifying them immediately. The situation concerned an annual support contract. They had paid for the 1996 fiscal year, but a second check for support was received 8 months before its due date. They were a government client and the practice of prepayment was not terribly uncommon. However, I should have contacted them immediately. The pressure of meeting payroll made it easier to credit their account for 1997 as opposed to calling them and giving them an option of having the check returned. The client caught the error and called for an explanation. I explained that we had credited their account through 1997. There was an awkward silence as this very important client became, justifiably, suspicious.   My dishonesty placed our professional relationship in jeopardy. I apologized and hung up. I will never make that mistake again. I went to see them the next day to admit that I had made a mistake. I apologized and told him that his trust was as important to me personally as his business was to our company. He thanked me for my honesty and our relationship took a step forward.

Never over-bill your customers. If you do over-bill and they pay you, give them a refund immediately. Nine times out of ten, the customer is not going to catch this, but if you catch it and bring it to their attention, you will have a customer for life.

Trust your swing to carry the river on the 11th hole of the Robert Trent Jones Golf Club. Manassas, Virginia.

Access to confidential information is a privilege that should be rewarded with confidentiality.

As I wrote this chapter, I thought how ridiculous it is. To remember to be honest. (Oh yeah, and don't kill anybody.) It must mean it is easier to lie than to do what it takes to make the truth look good. Do what it takes, it's great business.

"98 out of 100 of the rich men in America are honest.
That is why they are rich."
- Russell Herman Conwell, Founder,
Temple University

Golfers that cheat are pitiful. Do you look forward to playing golf with people who cheat? Of course not. There are two kinds of cheaters. Those that "accidentally" cheat because they do not know the rules of golf. And the real cheaters.

The rules of golf can be confusing and sometimes ridiculous. Learning the rules comes with time. The rest of your group may not understand that you do not know the rules, so never be afraid to ask for a ruling. I have seen the rules blatantly abused and take no pleasure in being the golf police. If a situation arises where no one in the group can specifically determine the ruling, play 2 balls and have the pro decide the proper scoring method.

In a friendly wager, it is not uncommon to play by local rules that bend the formal rules of golf. For instance, *Paradise* refers to the ability to improve your lie anywhere on the course. *Winter Rules* allow the lie to be improved only when you are in the fairway. Determine with your group which rules that you are choosing to bend for the day!

If you cheat in golf, you will cheat in life. If you cheat in life, you miss the whole boat. People do not have to see you cheat, they can feel it. If you are in the woods, and you can just as easily drop a ball as find yours, fight the urge, because people will eventually know. Trust me.

> *"Be more concerned with your character than with your reputation. Your character is what you really are while your reputation is merely what others think you are."*
> *- John Wooden, NCAA Basketball coach*

Keep yourself honest when giving putts. In a friendly game, giving putts is acceptable. When somebody gives you a putt that is clearly not a "gimme" say, "Thanks, but I've been missing the short ones. I could use the confidence." It is a great way to improve your game and show your character. Remember, if it is a "gimme", there's no excuse for missing it.

Never take a "do-over." It's a weak move. Hit a provisional if your ball might be lost or out of bounds. It removes the tendency to not play by the rules.

If you cheat, stop now. It will cost too much outside of the golf course. It may have already. Compromising your reputation for a game is silly and expensive. There are so many opportunities on the golf course to show your true colors. You can be friendly, honest, generous, and entertaining. People are paying more attention than you think.

It is also important to play by the rules and count your strokes to chart your improvement. Improvement is a common goal to all of us. If you are not counting your strokes properly, your improvement becomes a mystery. Swing the club. Count a stroke. Simple stuff. Moreover, nobody really cares how good or bad you are (or if you shoot 98 or 96). Use golf as a vehicle to show your honesty and integrity.

Remember that dishonesty, at some point, will be revealed. Whatever cash or hardware you win will not compensate for the losses of what you, unknowingly, lose by the act of cheating. There is power in honesty.

"Always tell the truth - it's the easiest
thing to remember."
-David Mamet, Playwright, Author of, among others,
<u>The Postman Always Rings Twice</u>, <u>Glengarry Glen Ross</u>

Club House ➡

Honesty

18 just doesn't scratch the itch while looking over the seductive opening holes of the European Club. "Emergency 9" anyone? Near Dublin, Ireland.

NUMBER 19 - THE GOOD HOOK

"It is better to give than receive."
- Santa Claus, CEO, Christmas

I know you were only expecting *18 Holes of Success* but we all know the best rounds end on the 19th. To make the experience true to life, get ready for Number 19. The 19th is where you relive your best and worst shots and unwind with your group. This is my favorite hole. Not because the beer is cold, which it is, but because it is your foursome without the golf. The 19th hole is pure camaraderie and the perfect setting for the "Good Hook." The lessons to be learned on this hole include the value of building relationships with everyone you come in contact with and the myriad of positive effects that those new relationships will have on you. In between bites of your sandwich you'll learn that treating everyone like a VIP is the best way to get the VIP treatment. Pass the beer nuts and popcorn and I will show you how new acquaintances are our most valuable investments. So total your scores, get the golf tournament on TV, settle the bets, and order another round while I motivate you to develop a personal relationship with everyone. And if you take my advice, your next beer may be on the house!

The "good hook" is a true art form. We all know someone that has a connection wherever they go. They get reservations, tee times, and free stuff. They are only a phone call away from the best tickets or the best party. How do those people do it? Well, its not that complicated and what this 19th hole is all about.

I learned a lot of these techniques from my older brother. He is a pro at this. He has included me on tons of free golf outings and always has plenty of people who owe him favors - it's unbelievable. I watch what he does and have added a few of my own techniques.

hooked (hookt) v. [Slang] given preferential treatment [*free ride, reduced fare, comped, free pass, free drinks, no cover charge, anything but retail*] see also, **hooked up**
          good hook n. [Slang] one who "hooks you up"

Getting "Hooked Up." Hopefully you have heard the term "hooked up." If you have not heard the term, maybe you have not been "hooked up," which is too bad. A "good hook" is your favorite bartender, who, after drinking all night, hands you a five-dollar tab. Of course you will leave $50 for what was probably a $30 tab.

In this situation, everybody wins. You end up paying a premium for the freedom to pay whatever you want. In other words, you pay your check on your terms. You feel great about leaving a better tip and are, happily, paying for that freedom. Your generosity is only limited by your conscience. The bartender ultimately gets a better tip and the bar gets a client that will refer his friends and certainly be back. Of course you may get a free drink from time to time, but the smart bartenders and bar owners subscribe to this theory for their better clients. So do the best business minds.

"Giving people a little more than they expect is a good way to get back a lot more than you expect."
-Robert Half, pioneer of specialized and temporary staffing, founder, Robert Half Industries

I also want to clarify that getting "hooked up" is not deceptive or dishonest. The concept is deeper than just getting a discount at someone else's expense. The "good hook" is an investment in a long-term relationship. If you get a $5 tab and leave $6, you are missing the point and will never be the person with all of the connections.

Win-Win-Feel the love! The "good hook" takes win-win to a new level. More like win-win-feel the love! People who get "hooked up" are people who focus on making friends and know that people enjoy doing favors. There are plenty of instances where people can offer you something free, put you at the top of the waiting list, or charge you a member's fee when you're not a member. We all do that, when we can, for the special people on our list. Nevertheless, before you can get "hooked up", a **personal** relationship must exist.

Raise your glass to friends and fun — the 19th is your hole-in-one! 19th hole, everywhere.

Lead with kindness. To understand this further, a perfect example concerns getting a tee time at your local course or club. The pro or starter usually controls the tee sheet and has some leverage one way or another. The best investment you can make is to bring that person a cold drink on a hot day or spend 10 minutes talking to them when you **do not** need a tee time. Pretty soon you may find that the starter only works on weekends and is actually a retired executive in your industry. Not only are you going to find yourself moved up a few notches on the tee sheet, you may find yourself in that elusive client's office who happens to be "Starter Steve's" good buddy.

Surprise! It is what you don't know about people that will surprise you the most. People of all walks of life consistently surprise me with mutual friends and similar experiences and interests. This is another reason to develop relationships with everyone. The worst thing that can happen when you attempt to develop a relationship with anyone is that you will brighten his or her day.

Talk to everybody. Get to know the person who helps you bag your groceries with the same enthusiasm as the Vice President who can approve your raise. Speak to people as their equal. Do not talk down to the ditch diggers and do not kiss-up to the CEOs. If anything, do the opposite. When meeting new people, kick off the relationship by speaking to them as if they are the only one in the room. This will not go unnoticed and is a good idea when speaking to anyone.

Beggars don't get hooked up. When meeting someone for the first time you do not want to have your hand out. It's dangerous and transparent to go into new relationships with your motivation being to get something free. The goal is to make a new friend. Be genuinely interested in having more friends, and the "hooks" will fall into place.

"There is a wonderful mythical law of nature that the three things we crave most in life - happiness, freedom, and peace of mind - are always attained by giving them to someone else."
- Peyton Conway March, U.S. Army officer, Spanish American War

Maximize transactions. There are reasons why some people get "hooked up", and others pay retail. A great source for new connections concerns maximizing the relationships encountered with any purchase that you make. If you're buying it now, you may buy it again. Get to know everyone associated with the transaction. Know their names and make sure they know yours. For example, introduce yourself to the managers of the restaurants you enjoy. It's easy. Talk about their menu; talk about how much you like their food and atmosphere. The next time you visit, who is not going to be impressed when the manager stops by your table and knows your name? It's no surprise that your check may be a little lower and your service a little better. Don't you think the staff is going to give a little extra service to the boss's good friend? Mark it down.

'Tis better to hook. Getting "hooked up" is great, but "hooking up" a new friend is better. Following through on a generous gesture is underestimated in its value to the soul. If you get "hooked" you must "hook." Identify a few things you can offer so you can take care of people who take care of you. The basic driving force is that favors will be offered when the opportunity presents itself. Always ask the question, "What can I do for you?" and be prepared to actually do something.

Small gifts are great tokens of appreciation. Send gifts to anyone who helps you for any reason. Have a gift drawer that contains small gifts from your travels or business. A bottle of wine, ball markers, hats, or golf shirts from the sale rack from far away courses all make great, inexpensive gifts. When buying inexpensive, interesting tokens, buy two and keep one for yourself and put the other in your gift drawer. Tell the recipient that you have one and now they have one and there are only two. Small gifts can germinate into large bonds.

Sending a thank you note is the best thing you can do to solidify a new relationship. It tells someone you care about him or her. Not the favor they did for you.

Barter. Informal bartering is a great way to exchange information and learn about someone else's business. People will do things for you because you take an interest in their business. People do not get "hooked up" strictly because they have favors owed to them. They are "hooked up" because there is a silent trust that grows as the relationship develops. If you do it right, it does not take long.

My attorney, Sam, and I have been friends for about ten years. We were paired by coincidence and met on the golf course. Over the first few holes I explained that I was starting a business and asked if he could recommend a lawyer who would be interested in handling some legal start-up work. He specialized in a different legal area but took the time to meet with my partner and me. We laid out our plans, and he said, "I like your plan, I'll take care of your legal documents, and get you set up." This was our first meeting. He "hooked us up" right off the bat. Now Sam was, and is, a very successful attorney. He was fantastic. He was also wise enough to know that, at the time, we did not have any money. He knew that if he took care of us now, we would take care of him later. That is the concept of the "hook." Sam took care of every legal issue of our business for the first seven years, and he never sent us a bill. Sam and I have become fantastic friends. He orchestrated the sale of the business and finally got paid. He's been a great friend over the years, and I can't wait to take care of Sam when the opportunity presents itself.

Money should be secondary. If you want to get "hooked up," avoid money as the driving factor. The "I'll scratch your back if you scratch mine" philosophy should rule. In some cases this does include a discount, but because you are a valued person or client, not because you are going to slip "a little something" to them in the parking lot. It is okay to tip the folks who are taking care of you, but you want to make sure they are not taking care of you primarily for the money. You want them to "hook you up" because they like you. When you take care of somebody make sure you are doing it for the satisfaction you get from doing someone a favor.

"Money is no good if you use it just as a weapon...if you share it, you'll always have enough. And if you don't, you'll never have enough."
- Chi Chi Rodriguez, Professional Golfer

Unfortunately, there are no "good hooks" on the golf course. A soft draw, maybe, but not a hook. However, the best golf is free golf. If a pro or assistant ever "hooks you up," make sure you do something nice for them. Tip them or at least buy some merchandise in the shop. Most assistants are in the training stages of their careers and do not make much money, so anything you can do is appreciated. Do not waste an opportunity to take care of those people who are taking care of you on the links.

Now you have no excuse for not having a connection when I come to town. Thanks for "hooking me up" and checking out my book. I hope it unlocks a few doors for you.

I enjoyed the round — good luck, until we meet again.

THE MAKING OF THIS BOOK

Have you ever wanted to write a book but didn't know where to start? I found myself in that position as I sought to include my passions into my next career. After years of deja vu on the golf course and in the office, the book topic was the easy part, what to do next was a puzzle. Defining and dissecting passion into components is a foreign process.

I took a shot in the dark and decided that at least 24 concepts or holes would be a great start to ultimately choose the best 18, at which point I decided 19 was a must. At that moment, the creative seed was planted. The challenge of defining 24 concepts took about a week. Now what? Visualization helps me act, so I typed each of the 24 chapter topics on the top of a sheet of paper and then typed **Business:** on the top half and **Golf:** on the bottom half. The 24 pieces of paper were then taped on the wall in my home office and I stared for a few months.

As ideas came, they were logged on their appropriate hole. On rainy or cold days, I brainstormed. On nice days I played golf. The ideas gradually filled the wall and the final 19 concepts came to life. I removed each "hole" from the wall and rambled into a tape recorder covering each of the topics with stories and ideas. Whatever came to mind was recorded as I pretended to tell a stranger why these ideas could be beneficial. My objective was for the book to read as if we were chatting during a round of golf.

The 19 monologs were then transcribed into a text document. The ideas were now in my computer and the translation process of these conversations into something that could be absorbed in successive chapters began.

Simultaneously, and before conceptualizing each hole, I began taking pictures of memorable golf holes. I did not own a camera so I bought the cardboard disposable kind and started clicking away. After the first few golf trips, I bought a point and shoot 35mm camera, however, the disposable cameras work quite well and a few shots in the book were taken with the camera at the bottom of the food chain. I photographed and edited a very rough draft.

As the book progressed I asked friends that seemed interested if they would help me edit my first draft. A year and a half after conception, the first version, complete with black and white photographs, and a plastic GBC binding was mailed to the group recovering from their twisted arms. The package included a questionnaire for suggestions on a variety of topics. I was pleasantly surprised at the amount of time people put into the manuscript, the overwhelming encouragement, and the creativity of ideas. I added my ideas to the inflow of suggestions and a *lengthy* to-do list was completed for each chapter.

Reconstructing each hole was the point at which the project felt like work. Intimidating work. After a year of rewriting, my new wife and I took a trip around the world, played golf, took photographs, gained perspective, and added the finishing touches and stories for the book.

After my best effort was completed, Brian McAndrew heard about the project and said he would be delighted to edit the manuscript. He is a published author, editor for *The Toronto Star,* and the brother-in-law of close friends. I then had a book that was, at least, grammatically correct. All I needed now was to get the product out before someone else. My idea seemed safe after looking for potential competition in the golf and self-improvement sections of book stores. My attorney took care of the copyright issues and the final challenge was getting the photographs and story to explode off of the pages.

Very early in the process I secured the website www.18holesofsuccess.com and had a small site teed up on the web until I was ready to use it. Darin Wardwell set it up and he and I stayed in touch. He had a few ideas for the layout that he wanted to share with me.

Around this time another friend of mine who had retired from the printing business walked me through the ABC's of printing a book. He recommended a printer and set up a meeting to tour their facility. They put together a quote and the numbers made sense.

The good news was up to this point I had spent very little money. A little on photography costs and postage but only a few hundred dollars at most. Darin's artistic suggestions blew me away. I shot a few more photos for the artwork and Darin worked his magic.

Everything in the book has a purpose. The blueprints in the background are from golf courses and various construction projects and were used to remind the reader that this book is a blueprint for their own success. The business quotes are supported artistically with golf graphics and the golf quotes are supported with business graphics further tying the two together. The chapter titles are engraved into plaques using a font (letter shape) found on U.S. paper currency for obvious reasons.

Patience played a major role and I found support everywhere. The staff of Kings Creek Country Club winced when they saw me come in with my camera. They prepared the food and set up the scenes that created the elegance and mouth watering appeal of *The Turn* and the *19th Hole*.

Three years after conception a press proof (test print) of a single chapter passed with flying colors. The artwork for the rest of the book was completed. The final press proof passed after a tweak or two and we were ready to rip film, make plates, and print. I stroked the check and what happens next is anybody's guess. I hope it sells but I really hope it helps.